VISUALIZING SECURED TRANSACTIONS

LexisNexis Law School Publishing Advisory Board

Charles B. Craver
Freda H. Alverson Professor of Law
The George Washington University Law School

Richard D. Freer
Robert Howell Hall Professor of Law
Emory University School of Law

Craig Joyce
Andrews Kurth Professor of Law &
Co-Director, Institute for Intellectual Property and Information Law
University of Houston Law Center

Ellen S. Podgor
Professor of Law &
Associate Dean of Faculty Development and Distance Education
Stetson University College of Law

Paul F. Rothstein
Professor of Law
Georgetown University Law Center

Robin Wellford Slocum
Professor of Law & Director, Legal Research and Writing Program
Chapman University School of Law

Charles J. Tabb
Alice Curtis Campbell Professor of Law
University of Illinois College of Law

Judith Welch Wegner
Professor of Law
University of North Carolina School of Law

VISUALIZING SECURED TRANSACTIONS

Laura B. Bartell
Professor of Law
Wayne State University Law School

Library of Congress Cataloging-in-Publication Data

Bartell, Laura B.
    Visualizing Secured Transactions / Laura B. Bartell
      p. cm.
    Includes index.
    ISBN 978-1-4224-1551-1 (softbound)
  1. Security (Law)—United States. 2. Actions and defenses—United States. I. Title.
    KF1050.B37 2007
    346.7307'4--dc22   2007035920

This publication is designed to provide accurate and authoritative information in regard to the subject matter covered. It is sold with the understanding that the publisher is not engaged in rendering legal, accounting, or other professional services. If legal advice or other expert assistance is required, the services of a competent professional should be sought.

LexisNexis and the Knowledge Burst logo are trademarks of Reed Elsevier Properties Inc, used under license. Matthew Bender is a registered trademark of Matthew Bender Properties Inc.

Copyright © 2007 Matthew Bender & Company, Inc., a member of the LexisNexis Group.
All Rights Reserved.

No copyright is claimed in the text of statutes, regulations, and excerpts from court opinions quoted within this work. Permission to copy material exceeding fair use, 17 U.S.C. § 107, may be licensed for a fee of 10¢ per page per copy from the Copyright Clearance Center, 222 Rosewood Drive, Danvers, Mass. 01923, telephone (978) 750-8400.

NOTE TO USERS
To ensure that you are using the latest materials available in this area, please be sure to periodically check the LexisNexis Law School web site for downloadable updates and supplements at www.lexisnexis.com/lawschool

Editorial Offices
744 Broad Street, Newark, NJ 07102 (973) 820-2000
201 Mission St., San Francisco, CA 94105-1831 (415) 908-3200
701 East Water Street, Charlottesville, VA 22902-7587 (434) 972-7600
www.lexis.com

To Stan, Joanna and Jeremy, whose love sustains me.
LBB

PREFACE

Article 9 of the Uniform Commercial Code was drafted with great care and in a way that was designed to provide certainty in the commercial markets. It was not written to provide ease of understanding.

In the course of teaching secured transactions over many years, I have found that students find it easier to grasp the substance of Article 9 if it is organized in a visual way. This is hardly surprising. Many of those who have made a study of learning have concluded that visual tools are useful in organizing ideas in a way that enables students to understand them and remember them. The brain responds to and recalls pictures in a way unrivaled by its response to the written word. When lectures or presentations are supported by visual aids, they are not only more interesting to watch, but the audience is likely to remember more about them.

Law students, perhaps even more than the population at large, seem to be genetically driven to seek structure in learning. Perhaps it is the desire to make sense out of a chaotic world that brings them to law school in the first place. Although I have found them generally averse to anything requiring the use of numbers or math, they blossom when given a flow chart or diagram. Even when I am teaching a statutory course as complex and foreign as secured transactions, when I package the concepts into one-page visual forms, complaints about reading the statute disappear because they can see how it fits into a larger picture (quite literally).

With that background, I have prepared this handbook of the many charts I have developed over the years to teach the basic concepts of Article 9 included in a secured transactions course. They are organized in chapters that correspond to the sections of the course I teach, rather than the organization of Article 9 itself. However, I have included visualizations of some material I do not teach in the hope that it may be helpful to others.

TABLE OF CONTENTS

Chapter 1 SCOPE 1

Chapter 2 CLASSIFICATION 11

Chapter 3 ATTACHMENT 23

Chapter 4 PERFECTION 31
- A. AUTOMATIC PERFECTION 32
- B. PERFECTION BY POSSESSION OR DELIVERY 36
- C. PERFECTION BY CONTROL 39
- D. PERFECTION BY COMPLIANCE WITH OTHER LAW 46
- E. PERFECTION BY FILING 46
  1. What Do You File? 47
  2. Who Is Permitted to File? 61
  3. What Does It Mean to File? 62
  4. Where Do You File? 63

Chapter 5 CHOICE OF LAW 65

Chapter 6 PRIORITY 75
- A. BASIC RULES OF PRIORITY 75
  1. Secured Creditors 75
  2. Lien Creditors 76
  3. Buyers 77
  4. Lessees or Licensees 82
- B. SPECIAL PRIORITY RULES 84
  1. Purchase-Money Security Interests 84
  2. Future Advances 86
  3. Control Collateral 88
  4. Purchasers of Chattel Paper or Instruments .. 89
  5. Transfers of Money 91
  6. Possessory Liens 92
  7. Fixtures 93
  8. Accessions 101
  9. Commingled Goods 102
  10. Right of Set-Off or Recoupment 103
  11. Federal Tax Liens 104

Chapter 7 BANKRUPTCY 113
    A. IMPACT OF BANKRUPTCY PETITION 113
    B. DETERMINATION OF SECURED STATUS 114
    C. POST-PETITION EFFECT OF SECURITY INTEREST 116
    D. TREATMENT OF COLLATERAL DURING BANKRUPTCY CASE 117
    E. AVOIDING POWERS 120
        1. Avoidance of Lien Impairing Exemption 120
        2. Strong-Arm Clause 122
        3. Fraudulent Transfer or Obligation 123
        4. Preference 126
    F. TREATMENT OF SECURED CLAIM 133
        1. Chapter 7 134
        2. Chapter 13 137
        3. Chapter 11 138

Chapter 8 DISPOSITION OF COLLATERAL AND PROCEEDS 141

Chapter 9 RIGHTS AND DUTIES OF SECURED PARTY 151

Chapter 10 RIGHTS OF THIRD PARTIES 155

Chapter 11 DEFAULT AND REMEDIES 161
    A. ENFORCEMENT OF SECURITY INTEREST 161
        1. Judicial Enforcement 162
        2. Collection and Enforcement 163
        3. Right to Take Possession 165
        4. Disposition of Collateral 166
        5. Acceptance in Satisfaction of Obligation 173
    B. RIGHTS AND REMEDIES OF DEBTOR AND THIRD PARTIES 176
        1. Redemption 176
        2. Remedies for Non-compliance 177
        3. Remedies Relating to Deficiency 180

Chapter 12 TRANSITION RULES 185

Table of Statutes TS-1

Index I-1

Chapter 1
SCOPE

The term "scope" deals with whether a particular transaction is governed by Article 9 of the Uniform Commercial Code (UCC) or not. If a transaction does not fall within the scope of Article 9, this does not mean that the transaction is illegal or immoral or otherwise impermissible. It simply means that Article 9 is not applicable to its validity or effect.

Section 9-109 defines the scope of Article 9. Clause (a) of that section is called "General scope of article" and sets forth six different types of transactions that fall within the ambit of Article 9. In fact, the first one listed is the true general scope provision defining what most people would call a "secured transaction." The other five paragraphs sweep into Article 9 transactions that are not "secured transactions" in the classic sense, but that the drafters have brought into the scope of Article 9 for policy reasons.

The following chart visualizes the general scope provision of § 9-109(a).

SCOPE OF ARTICLE 9 § 9-109(a)	
GENERAL SCOPE	**ADDITIONAL INCLUSIONS**
TRANSACTION THAT CREATES A SECURITY INTEREST § 1-201(b)(35) IN PERSONAL PROPERTY OR FIXTURES § 9-102(a)(41) BY CONTRACT § 1-201(b)(12)	1) AGRICULTURAL LIEN § 9-102(a)(5) 2) SALE OF ACCOUNTS § 9-102(a)(2), CHATTEL PAPER § 9-102(a)(11), PAYMENT INTANGIBLES § 9-102(a)(61), OR PROMISSORY NOTES § 9-102(a)(65) 3) CONSIGNMENT § 9-102(a)(20) 4) ART. 2 OR 2A SECURITY INTEREST 5) ART. 4 OR 5 SECURITY INTEREST

Although many definitions used in Article 9 will be visualized in connection with the analysis of classification of collateral, some of the terms used in the general scope provision may be examined more closely now.

The first term essential to understanding the scope of Article 9 is "security interest," which is defined not in Article 9 but in Article 1 of the Uniform Commercial Code. Section 1-201(b)(35) has a general definition in the first sentence that expresses the normal understanding of a security interest. It then adds a second sentence describing additional interests to be included that are not within the normal understanding, but that mirror the additional transactions picked up by the general scope provision in paragraphs (3) and (4) of § 9-109(a). The next two sentences exclude certain Article 2 interests from the definition. The penultimate sentence adds the retention of title to goods sold to the buyer, the absence of which would provide sellers ready means to avoid complying with the requirements of Article 9 while retaining priority to goods in the hands of buyers. The final sentence contrasts security interests with leases, and directs us to a separate section, § 1-203, for guidance on making the distinction. A visualization of the definition of "security interest" follows.

SECURITY INTEREST § 1-201(b)(35)		
GENERAL DEFINITION	INCLUSIONS	EXCLUSIONS
INTEREST IN PERSONAL PROPERTY OR FIXTURES § 9-102(a)(41) WHICH SECURES PAYMENT OR PERFORMANCE OF AN OBLIGATION	INTEREST OF CONSIGNOR § 9-102(a)(21) INTEREST OF BUYER OF ACCOUNTS § 9-102(a)(2), CHATTEL PAPER § 9-102(a)(11), PAYMENT INTANGIBLE § 9-102(a)(61), PROMISSORY NOTE § 9-102(a)(65) IN ART. 9 TRANSACTION RETENTION OR RESERVATION OF TITLE BY SELLER OF GOODS	SPECIAL PROPERTY INTEREST OF BUYER OF GOODS UPON IDENTIFICATION UNDER § 2-401 RIGHT OF SELLER OR LESSOR OF GOODS TO RETAIN OR ACQUIRE POSSESSION UNDER ART. 2 OR 2A

Because the definition of "security interest" tells us that we have to distinguish security interests from leases, we must also look at § 1-203 if we want to understand what a "security interest" is. Section 1-203(a) first tells us that deciding whether a transaction that looks like a lease is in fact a lease, or is instead a security interest in disguise, is a question of fact.

Section 1-203(b) then describes circumstances under which a transaction will be determined to be a security interest despite its form as a lease, that is, when a confluence of circumstances are determinative in characterizing the transaction as one creating a security interest. Section 1-203(c) tells us facts that, by contrast, are not determinative (although, of course, a court may consider the existence of such facts in making its factual determination). Because the term "nominal additional consideration" is an important factor in establishing whether a lease or security interest exists, § 1-203(d) defines that term for us.

A visualization of the provisions distinguishing a lease from a security interest in § 1-203 follows.

LEASE/SECURITY INTEREST GUIDELINES § 1-203	
NOT DETERMINATIVE	MUST BE SECURED SALE

1) PRESENT VALUE OF CONSIDERATION $\geq$ FMV AT TIME OF LEASING
 	
2) LESSEE ASSUMES RISK OF LOSS, PAYS TAXES, MAINTAINS, ETC.
 	
3) LESSEE HAS OPTION TO RENEW OR PURCHASE
 	
4) LESSEE HAS OPTION TO RENEW AT RENT $\geq$ FMV OF RENT AT TIME
 	
5) LESSEE HAS OPTION TO PURCHASE AT PRICE $\geq$ FMV OF GOODS AT TIME
	1) CONSIDERATION PAID FOR LEASE TERM NOT SUBJECT TO TERMINATION BY LESSEE
	
	AND
	
	2) LESSEE GETS FULL ECONOMIC LIFE OF GOODS BY
	
	   A) ORIGINAL TERM $\geq$ REMAINING ECONOMIC LIFE, OR
	
	   B) REQUIRED RENEWALS FOR REMAINING ECONOMIC LIFE OR REQUIRED PURCHASE, OR
	
	   C) OPTIONAL RENEWAL FOR REMAINING ECONOMIC LIFE FOR $\leq$ NOMINAL CONSIDERATION*
	
	   D) OPTIONAL PURCHASE FOR $\leq$ NOMINAL CONSIDERATION*
	
	* NOMINAL CONSIDERATION
	
	= LESS THAN REASONABLY PREDICTABLE COST OF PERFORMING LEASE IF OPTION NOT EXERCISED
	
	$\neq$ FAIR MARKET VALUE (FMV) OF RENT OR GOODS AT TIME OPTION EXERCISED

Returning to the general scope provision, § 9-109(a), three other special transactions that are listed as within the scope of Article 9 require further scrutiny before we look at the exceptions and exclusions from scope. The first is "agricultural lien."

An "agricultural lien" is a type of non-possessory statutory lien on farm products (a term discussed in Chapter 2). It was incorporated in the scope of Article 9 to facilitate agricultural financing. Agricultural liens have five distinguishing features: (1) what property they attach to, (2) what obligations they secure, (3) who holds them, (4) how they are created, and (5) their non-possessory nature (compare "possessory lien" in § 9-333(a)).

A visualization of the definition of "agricultural lien" follows.

AGRICULTURAL LIEN § 9-102(a)(5)				
IN WHAT PROPERTY	FOR WHAT OBLIGATIONS	HOLDER	HOW CREATED	POSSESSORY OR NON-POSSESSORY
FARM PRODUCTS § 9-102(a)(34)	GOODS OR SERVICES FURNISHED IN CONNECTION WITH FARMING OPERATION § 9-102(a)(35), OR RENT ON REAL PROPERTY LEASED IN CONNECTION WITH FARMING OPERATION	FURNISHER OF GOODS OR SERVICES IN ORDINARY COURSE OF BUSINESS, OR LESSOR OF REAL PROPERTY	STATUTE	NON-POSSESSORY

A second specific inclusion in the scope of Article 9 is for sales of accounts, chattel paper, payment intangibles, or promissory notes. The definitions of those terms are discussed in Chapter 2. However, even a "true sale" of those types of property is covered by Article 9 in order to avoid the problem of distinguishing between sales and secured transactions involving such assets. However, as described in the exclusions to scope in § 9-109(d), discussed later in this chapter, Article 9 is inapplicable to some sales and assignments of these types of property that "by their nature, do not concern commercial financing transactions." Official Comment 12 to § 9-109.

The inclusion of these sales in the scope of Article 9 does not mean that, as between the seller and buyer of those assets, the seller retains any interest in them after a sale. § 9-318(a). However, if the buyer's "security interest" in those assets is not perfected, see Chapter 4, a subsequent creditor or "purchaser," § 1-201(b)(30), may obtain rights in the sold assets from the debtor to the same extent as if the sale had not occurred. § 9-319.

A visualization of the scope provision relating to sales of accounts, chattel paper, payment intangibles and promissory notes follows:

SCOPE PROVISIONS RELATING TO SALES OF ACCOUNTS, CHATTEL PAPER, PAYMENT INTANGIBLES AND PROMISSORY NOTES

INCLUDED § 9-109(a)(3)	EXCLUDED § 9-109(d)(4) - (7)
SALE OF ACCOUNTS, CHATTEL PAPER, PAYMENT INTANGIBLES, OR PROMISSORY NOTES	1) SALE AS PART OF SALE OF BUSINESS OUT OF WHICH THEY AROSE 2) ASSIGNMENT FOR PURPOSE OF COLLECTION ONLY 3) ASSIGNMENT OF RIGHT TO PAYMENT UNDER CONTRACT TO NEW PERFORMING PARTY 4) ASSIGNMENT OF SINGLE ACCOUNT, PAYMENT INTANGIBLE OR PROMISSORY NOTE IN SATISFACTION OF PREEXISTING INDEBTEDNESS

"Consignments" are also included in the scope of Article 9. A consignment is traditionally described as a transaction in which an owner of goods delivers them to a third party for the purpose of sale to the public without an intention to transfer title to the goods unless and until that sale is consummated. In other words, it is a bailment for the purpose of sale. Such a transaction should be distinguished from those described in § 2-326(1), the sale on approval (when the buyer of goods receives goods the buyer intends to use on trial and tests them before agreeing to accept them) and the sale or return (when the buyer of goods accepts them intending to resell them, but the seller agrees to take them back in lieu of payment in the event the buyer is unable to do so). It should also be distinguished from a secured transaction, in which an owner of goods sells the goods on credit to a buyer, taking back a security interest in the goods to secure the obligation to pay the purchase price.

But the form of a consignment may also be used to mask what is in substance a secured transaction. These "consignments intended for security," as Official Comment 14 to § 9-102 describes consignments that are really surreptitious secured transactions, are included in the scope of Article 9 by the general scope provision of § 9-109(a)(1) ("a transaction, regardless of its form, that creates a security interest").

Even true consignments, those that are not secured transactions in consignment clothing, separate possession of goods (by the consignee) from ownership (in the consignor), which has the potential to mislead creditors of the consignee. Therefore, true consignments are included in the scope of Article 9 if they fall within the definition of "consignment" in § 9-102(a)(20).

The definition sets out six requirements for a consignment to qualify as an Article 9 "consignment." Three relate to the "consignee," that is, the merchant to which the seller has consigned goods for sale. § 9-102(a)(19). The merchant must use a name other than the seller's name, cannot be an auctioneer, and must not be generally known by its creditors to be substantially engaged in selling goods of others. Two other requirements for an Article 9 "consignment" are designed to exclude transactions in which compliance with Article 9 filing requirements is "inappropriate or of insufficient benefit to justify the costs." Official Comment 14 to § 9-102. For the consignment to be within the scope of Article 9, each delivery of goods must have a value of at least $1,000, and the goods may not be consumer goods (§ 9-102(a)(23)) immediately before the delivery. The final requirement is that the transaction is not a consignment intended for security. If it is, it falls within the scope of Article 9 in its own right and not as a "consignment."

A visualization of the definition of "consignment" follows:

CONSIGNMENT § 9-102(a)(20)			
MERCHANT/ CONSIGNEE: 1) DEALS IN GOODS UNDER NAME OTHER THAN CONSIGNOR'S NAME, 2) NOT AN AUCTIONEER, AND 3) NOT GENERALLY KNOWN BY CREDITORS TO BE SUBSTANTIALLY ENGAGED IN SELLING GOODS OF OTHERS	AGGREGATE VALUE OF GOODS IN EACH DELIVERY IS $1,000 OR MORE	GOODS ARE NOT CONSUMER GOODS § 9-102(a)(23) IMMEDIATELY BEFORE DELIVERY	TRANSACTION DOES NOT CREATE SECURITY INTEREST

If a consignment falls within the scope of Article 9, and the "consignor" does not perfect its "security interest" in the consigned goods, *see* Chapter 4, a creditor of the consignee may be able to acquire rights to the goods superior to those of the consignor. § 9-319.

In four situations described in § 9-109(c), Article 9 defers to other laws to the extent they are applicable to a particular transaction. These include federal laws, regulations and treaties to the extent they preempt the state-enacted UCC, and statutes of the enacting state, and of other states, foreign countries, or governmental units (§ 9-102(a)(45)) of those bodies, to the extent they expressly govern security interests of those entities.

In thirteen other situations described in § 9-109(d), Article 9 is simply inapplicable to the transaction.

Even if an obligation is secured in a transaction that is excluded from the scope of Article 9, § 9-109(b) emphasizes that a security interest in that secured obligation may still be governed by Article 9. Thus, a security interest in an obligation secured by a mortgage is within the scope of Article 9 even though Article 9 was inapplicable to the transaction by which the obligation became secured by the mortgage (because it was a real property transaction). *See* Official Comment 7 to § 9-109.

A visualization of these limitations on the applicability of Article 9 follows:

EXCLUSIONS FROM ARTICLE 9	
EXCLUSIONS TO EXTENT OTHER LAW GOVERNS § 9-109(c)	EXCLUSIONS IN ALL CASES § 9-109(d)
1) FEDERAL STATUTES, REGULATIONS, TREATIES 2) ANOTHER STATUTE OF SAME STATE GOVERNING SECURITY INTERESTS CREATED BY STATE OR STATE GOVERNMENTAL UNIT 3) STATUTE OF ANOTHER STATE OR FOREIGN COUNTRY OR GOVERNMENTAL UNIT THEREOF GOVERNING SECURITY INTERESTS CREATED BY OTHER STATE OR COUNTRY OR GOVERNMENTAL UNIT THEREOF 4) RIGHTS OF TRANSFEREE BENEFICIARY UNDER LETTER OF CREDIT UNDER § 5-114	1) LANDLORD'S LIEN 2) STATUTORY OR COMMON LAW LIEN FOR SERVICES OR MATERIALS 3) WAGE ASSIGNMENTS 4) SALE OF ACCOUNTS, CHATTEL PAPER, PAYMENT INTANGIBLES OR PROMISSORY NOTES AS PART OF SALE OF BUSINESS 5) ASSIGNMENT OF ACCOUNTS, CHATTEL PAPER, PAYMENT INTANGIBLES OR PROMISSORY NOTES FOR COLLECTION ONLY 6) ASSIGNMENT OF RIGHT TO PAYMENT UNDER CONTRACT TO NEW PERFORMING PARTY 7) ASSIGNMENT OF SINGLE ACCOUNT, PAYMENT INTANGIBLE OR PROMISSORY NOTE IN SATISFACTION OF INDEBTEDNESS 8) TRANSFER OF INTEREST IN INSURANCE POLICY OR CLAIM 9) ASSIGNMENT OF RIGHT TO JUDGMENT 10) RIGHT OF RECOUPMENT OR SET-OFF 11) INTEREST IN REAL PROPERTY 12) ASSIGNMENT OF NON-COMMERCIAL TORT CLAIM 13) ASSIGNMENT OF DEPOSIT ACCOUNT IN CONSUMER TRANSACTION

Chapter 2
CLASSIFICATION

One of the most challenging aspects of secured transactions is gaining familiarity with the terminology. In particular, all of the types of property in which an Article 9 security interest may be created, called "collateral," § 9-102(a)(12), is given a label and definition (which may not necessarily comport with the dictionary definition of that label outside the commercial context).

All of the major categories of property that may become collateral are listed in the definition of "general intangible" in § 9-102(a)(42). The term "general intangible" is the catch-all definition, the label one gives to property if another definition does not apply. Specifically included in the definition is "payment intangibles" (defined in § 9-102(a)(61) as general intangibles under which the account debtor's principal obligation is to make a payment) and software (defined in § 9-102(a)(75) to mean computer programs and supporting information not embedded in goods). A sale of payment intangibles is within the scope of Article 9. § 9-109(a)(3).

A visualization of the definition of "general intangible" follows:

| GENERAL INTANGIBLE ||
| § 9-102(a)(42) ||
EXCLUDED	INCLUDED
ACCOUNTS CHATTEL PAPER COMMERCIAL TORT CLAIMS DEPOSIT ACCOUNTS DOCUMENTS GOODS INSTRUMENTS INVESTMENT PROPERTY LETTER-OF-CREDIT RIGHTS LETTERS OF CREDIT MONEY OIL, GAS, OR OTHER MINERALS BEFORE EXTRACTION	ANY OTHER PERSONAL PROPERTY, INCLUDING PAYMENT INTANGIBLES § 9-102(a)(61) AND SOFTWARE § 9-102(a)(75)

Each of the types of property excluded from the definition of "general intangibles" requires its own discussion.

The first exclusion is for "accounts," defined in § 9-102(a)(2). An account always represents a right to payment of a monetary obligation, whether or not earned by performance. The definition then lists ways in which this right to payment may arise to create an account. Specifically included are "health-care-insurance receivables," defined in § 9-102(a)(46) as an interest in or claim under an insurance policy which is a right to payment for health-care goods or services. The definition then sets forth six situations in which property that includes a right to payment does not fall within the definition of "account."

In most cases, a sale of accounts is within the scope of Article 9, even though it is a "true sale" rather than a secured transaction. § 9-109(a)(3).

A visualization of the definition of "account" follows:

ACCOUNT § 9-102(a)(2)	
RIGHT TO PAYMENT WHETHER OR NOT EARNED BY PERFORMANCE	
INCLUDED	EXCLUDED
1) FOR PROPERTY SOLD, LEASED, LICENSED, ASSIGNED OR DISPOSED OF 2) FOR SERVICES RENDERED 3) FOR POLICY OF INSURANCE ISSUED 4) FOR SECONDARY OBLIGATION INCURRED 5) FOR ENERGY PROVIDED 6) FOR CHARTER HIRE OF VESSEL 7) FOR USE OF CREDIT OR CHARGE CARD 8) AS LOTTERY WINNINGS 9) HEALTH-CARE-INSURANCE RECEIVABLES § 9-102(a)(46)	1) EVIDENCED BY CHATTEL PAPER OR INSTRUMENT 2) COMMERCIAL TORT CLAIMS 3) DEPOSIT ACCOUNTS 4) INVESTMENT PROPERTY 5) LETTER-OF-CREDIT RIGHTS OR LETTERS OF CREDIT 6) PAYMENT FOR MONEY OR FUNDS ADVANCED OTHER THAN BY CREDIT OR CHARGE CARD

The second category of property excluded from the definition of "general intangible" is "chattel paper," which is defined in § 9-102(a)(11). Chattel paper is unlike either general intangibles or accounts—which have no physical representation—in that it is embodied in a "record" or "records" (information in a tangible form or retrievable from electronic form, § 9-102(a)(69)). To be chattel paper, the record or records must evidence *BOTH* (1) a monetary obligation, and (2) a security interest in specific goods to secure that obligation (which may be coupled with a security interest in or license of software used in the goods) or lease of specific goods under which the monetary obligation arises (which may also be coupled with a license of software used in the goods). The definition goes on to enumerate two types of monetary obligations that are excluded from the definition (they are explicitly included in the definition of "account" in § 9-102(a)(2)).

Chattel paper is either "tangible chattel paper" if it is evidenced by a record or records in tangible form, § 9-102(a)(78), or "electronic chattel paper" if it is evidenced by a record or records in electronic form. § 9-102(a)(31). A sale of chattel paper is within the scope of Article 9. § 9-109(a)(3).

A visualization of the definition of "chattel paper" follows:

CHATTEL PAPER § 9-102(a)(11)		
INCLUDED		EXCLUDED
RECORD OR RECORDS IN TANGIBLE FORM ("TANGIBLE CHATTEL PAPER" § 9-102(a)(78)) OR ELECTRONIC FORM ("ELECTRONIC CHATTEL PAPER" § 9-102(a)(31)) EVIDENCING BOTH:		CONTRACT FOR USE OR HIRE OF VESSEL RIGHT TO PAYMENT FOR USE OF CREDIT OR CHARGE CARD
MONETARY OBLIGATION, AND	1) SECURITY INTEREST IN SPECIFIC GOODS (MAY INCLUDE SECURITY INTEREST IN OR LICENSE OF SOFTWARE USED IN GOODS), OR 2) LEASE OF SPECIFIC GOODS (MAY INCLUDE LICENSE OF SOFTWARE USED IN GOODS)	

The third exclusion from the definition of "general intangibles" is for "commercial tort claims," defined in § 9-102(a)(13). Recall that under the exclusions from the scope of Article 9 in § 9-109(d)(12), an assignment of claims arising in tort is generally not covered by Article 9 with the exception of commercial tort claims. A tort claim is always a "commercial tort claim" if it is held by an "organization" (which, according to § 1-201(b)(25) means a "person," defined in § 1-201(b)(27), other than an individual, such as a corporation, business trust, estate, trust, partnership, limited liability company, association, joint venture, government, governmental subdivision, agency, or instrumentality, public corporation, or any other legal or commercial entity). A tort claim is also a "commercial tort claim" if it is held by an individual, but the claim arose in the course of the individual's business or profession, and does not include damages for personal injury or death of an individual. A visualization of the definition of "commercial tort claim" follows:

COMMERCIAL TORT CLAIM § 9-102(a)(13)	
CLAIM ARISING IN TORT AND EITHER:	
CLAIMANT IS ORGANIZATION § 1-201(b)(25)	CLAIMANT IS INDIVIDUAL AND 1) CLAIM ARISE IN COURSE OF CLAIMANT'S BUSINESS OR PROFESSION, AND 2) CLAIM IS NOT FOR PERSONAL INJURY OR DEATH

The next exclusion from the definition of "general intangibles" is for "deposit accounts." We know from § 9-109(d)(13) that assignments of deposit accounts in consumer transactions, § 9-102(a)(26), are not in the scope of Article 9. However, in other secured transactions, security interests in deposit accounts are governed by Article 9. "Deposit account" is defined in § 9-102(a)(29) and includes any type of account maintained with a bank. Explicitly excluded are investment property (which would include accounts maintained with brokers) and accounts evidenced by an instrument (which would be "instruments," § 9-102(a)(47)). A visualization of the definition of "deposit account" follows:

DEPOSIT ACCOUNT § 9-102(a)(29)	
INCLUDED	EXCLUDED
DEMAND, TIME, SAVINGS, PASSBOOK, OR SIMILAR ACCOUNT MAINTAINED WITH A BANK	INVESTMENT PROPERTY ACCOUNT EVIDENCED BY INSTRUMENT

"Documents" are defined in § 9-102(a)(30) and are *not* any writing conveying information (as a non-lawyer might assume from the dictionary definition). Instead, "documents" are one of two types of specialized pieces of commercial documentation, the "document of title," defined in § 1-201(b)(16) and the subject of UCC Article 7, or receipts in the nature of warehouse receipts described in § 7-201(b). Documents of title are records that are issued by or to a bailee of goods and evidence the holder's right to receive, control, hold, and dispose of the record and the goods that the record covers. Typical documents of title include bills of lading, transport documents, dock warrants, dock receipts, warehouse receipts and orders for delivery of goods. A visualization of the definition of "document" follows:

DOCUMENT § 9-102(a)(30)		
DOCUMENT OF TITLE § 1-201(b)(16)		RECEIPT OF TYPE DESCRIBED IN § 7-201(b)
DEFINITION	EXAMPLES	RECEIPT FOR GOODS STORED UNDER STATUTE REQUIRING BOND AGAINST WITHDRAWAL OR LICENSE FOR ISSUANCE OF RECEIPTS
RECORD 1) IN REGULAR COURSE OF BUSINESS IS TREATED AS EVIDENCING RIGHT TO RECEIVE, CONTROL, HOLD AND DISPOSE OF GOODS, AND 2) ISSUED BY OR ADDRESSED TO BAILEE COVERING GOODS IN BAILEE'S POSSESSION	BILL OF LADING TRANSPORT DOCUMENT DOCK WARRANT DOCK RECEIPT WAREHOUSE RECEIPT ORDER FOR DELIVERY OF GOODS	

"Goods" are the tangible form of personal property with which most people are familiar. The definition in § 9-102(a)(44) defines "goods" as "all things that are movable when a security interest attaches." It then adds to the definition certain categories of property that are not strictly speaking movable, but are intended to be included. At the end of the definition the other categories of collateral are explicitly excluded; property can fall within one and only one classification for Article 9 purposes, and it does not fall within the term "goods" unless the other categories are not applicable.

A visualization of the definition of "goods" follows:

GOODS § 9-102(a)(44)	
ALL THINGS THAT ARE MOVABLE AT THE TIME THE SECURITY INTEREST ATTACHES	
INCLUDED	EXCLUDED
FIXTURES STANDING TIMBER TO BE CUT UNBORN YOUNG OF ANIMALS CROPS GROWN, GROWING OR TO BE GROWN MANUFACTURED HOMES COMPUTER PROGRAM EMBEDDED IN GOODS IF CUSTOMARILY CONSIDERED PART OF GOODS AND OWNER OF GOODS MAY USE IT	ACCOUNTS CHATTEL PAPER COMMERCIAL TORT CLAIMS DEPOSIT ACCOUNTS DOCUMENTS GENERAL INTANGIBLES INSTRUMENTS INVESTMENT PROPERTY LETTER-OF-CREDIT RIGHTS LETTERS OF CREDIT MONEY OIL, GAS OR OTHER MINERALS BEFORE EXTRACTION

The category of "goods" is divided into four subcategories: "consumer goods," "farm products," "inventory," and "equipment." The four subcategories are mutually exclusive. All goods fall into only one subcategory, although the goods may have a different classification depending on the use to which they are put by a different debtor. Thus, goods that constitute inventory in the hands of one debtor, a retailer, may be consumer goods in the hands of the purchaser of those goods, a consumer.

"Consumer goods" are goods used or bought for use primarily for personal, family or household purposes. § 9-102(a)(23).

Only a debtor engaged in a "farming operation" (defined in § 9-102(a)(35)) can have goods labeled as "farm products." Section 9-102(a)(34) includes in the definition crops, livestock, supplies and products of crops or livestock in their unmanufactured states. If goods qualify as "farm products," they are not "inventory."

"Inventory" is other goods held for sale or lease or to be furnished under a contract of service, as well as goods actually leased by a lessor or furnished under a contract of service, and raw materials, work in process, or materials used or consumer in a business. § 9-102(a)(48). Official Comment 4(a) to § 9-102 suggests that goods are inventory if they are used up or consumed in a business over a short period of time, but are equipment if they are fixed assets or have a relatively long life.

"Equipment" is goods that do not fall within any of the other three subcategories. § 9-102(a)(33).

A visualization of the subcategories of goods follows:

SUBCATEGORIES OF GOODS			
CONSUMER GOODS § 9-102(a)(23)	EQUIPMENT § 9-102(a)(33)	FARM PRODUCTS § 9-102(a)(34)	INVENTORY § 9-102(a)(48)
USED OR BOUGHT FOR USE PRIMARILY FOR PERSONAL, FAMILY OR HOUSEHOLD PURPOSES	GOODS OTHER THAN INVENTORY, FARM PRODUCTS, OR CONSUMER GOODS	DEBTOR IS ENGAGED IN FARMING OPERATION § 9-102(a)(35) AND: 1) CROPS (NOT STANDING TIMBER) 2) LIVESTOCK 3) SUPPLIES USED OR PRODUCED IN FARMING OPERATION, OR 4) UNMANUFACTURED PRODUCTS OF CROPS OR LIVESTOCK	NOT FARM PRODUCTS AND 1) LEASED BY LESSOR 2) HELD FOR SALE OR LEASE OR TO BE FURNISHED UNDER CONTRACT OF SERVICE 3) FURNISHED UNDER CONTRACT OF SERVICE, OR 4) RAW MATERIALS, WORK IN PROCESS, OR MATERIALS USED OR CONSUMED IN BUSINESS

The "instruments" referred to in Article 9 are not the type that create music. The definition in § 9-102(a)(47) includes two different types of writings. The first is a "negotiable instrument," defined in § 3-104. A typical example is a check written on a bank account. The second is any other writing that evidences a right to the payment of a monetary obligation, is not a security agreement or lease, and is of a type that in the ordinary course of business is transferred by delivery with any necessary indorsement or assignment. A typical example of this type of instrument is a "promissory note." § 9-102(a)(65). A sale of promissory notes is generally within the scope of Article

9. § 9-109(a)(3). The definition of "instrument" continues by excluding certain types of property that are included in other categories.

A visualization of the definition of "instrument" follows:

INSTRUMENT § 9-102(a)(47)	
NEGOTIABLE INSTRUMENT § 3-104: UNCONDITIONAL PROMISE OR ORDER TO PAY A FIXED AMOUNT 1) PAYABLE TO BEARER OR TO ORDER, 2) PAYABLE ON DEMAND OR AT DEFINITE TIME, AND 3) STATES NO OTHER UNDERTAKING OR INSTRUCTION	OTHER WRITING 1) EVIDENCES RIGHT TO PAYMENT OF MONETARY OBLIGATION, 2) *NOT* SECURITY AGREEMENT OR LEASE, AND 3) OF TYPE WHICH IN ORDINARY COURSE OF BUSINESS IS TRANSFERRED BY DELIVERY WITH ANY NECESSARY ENDORSEMENT
	EXCLUDING 1) INVESTMENT PROPERTY 2) LETTERS OF CREDIT 3) CREDIT CARD SLIPS

"Investment property" is also a term that defies intuitive understanding. It is *not* simply property in which someone invests. Rather, § 9-102(a)(49) provides five different subcategories of investment property: "security," "security entitlement," "securities account," "commodity contract," and "commodity account." Although Article 9 contains definitions for "commodity contract" and "commodity account," the other terms used in the definition of "investment property" are in Article 8.

A visualization of the definition of "investment property" follows:

INVESTMENT PROPERTY § 9-102(a)(49)				
SECURITY § 8-102(a)(15)	SECURITY ENTITLEMENT § 8-102(a)(17)	SECURITIES ACCOUNT § 8-501(a)	COMMODITY CONTRACT § 9-102(a)(15)	COMMODITY ACCOUNT § 9-102(a)(14)
OBLIGATION OF AN ISSUER OR INTEREST IN AN ISSUER	PROPERTY INTEREST OF PERSON IDENTIFIED IN RECORDS OF BANK OR BROKER OR OTHER SECURITIES INTERMEDIARY, § 8-102(a)(14)	ACCOUNT TO WHICH FINANCIAL ASSET MAY BE CREDITED	COMMODITY FUTURES CONTRACT, OPTION ON A COMMODITY FUTURES CONTRACT, COMMODITY OPTION OR SIMILAR CONTRACT	ACCOUNT MAINTAINED BY FUTURES COMMISSION MERCHANT OR OTHER COMMODITY INTERMEDIARY, § 9-102(a)(17), IN WHICH COMMODITY CONTRACT IS CARRIED FOR COMMODITY CUSTOMER, § 9-102(a)(16)
1) IN BEARER OR REGISTERED FORM OR TRANSFER MAY BE REGISTERED ON BOOKS,				
2) DIVISIBLE INTO CLASS OR SERIES OF SHARES, AND				
3) TYPE TRADED ON SECURITIES MARKETS				

"Letters of credit" are covered by Article 5 of the Uniform Commercial Code. As defined in § 5-102(a)(10), a letter of credit is a definite undertaking by an "issuer," § 5-102(a)(9), often a bank, to a "beneficiary," § 5-102(a)(3), at the request of an "applicant," § 5-102(a)(2). In the letter of credit, the issuer undertakes to make a payment or deliver something of value to the beneficiary if the beneficiary satisfies the conditions as described in the letter of credit.

The right to payment or performance under a letter of credit (but not the right of a beneficiary to *demand* payment or performance from the issuer) is called a "letter-of-credit right." § 9-102(a)(51).

"Money" is a medium of exchange currently authorized or adopted by a government. § 1-201(b)(24). In the United States, the dollar and its various subdivisions would constitute "money."

Minerals that may be extracted from the ground—such as oil, gas, coal, and the like—are treated as real property prior to their extraction, and personal property thereafter. Prior to their extraction, therefore, any interest that may be granted in the minerals is not subject to Article 9 under the general scope provision of § 9-109(a). Once the minerals are removed from the real property, they are labeled "as-extracted collateral," § 9-102(a)(6), and would be included in the definition of "goods." *See* Official Comment 4(c) to § 9-102.

Chapter 3
ATTACHMENT

In most cases, a security interest "attaches" to collateral when it is enforceable as a contractual matter between the debtor and the secured party. The "debtor" is defined in § 9-102(a)(28) as the person having an interest in the collateral, the seller of accounts, chattel paper, payment intangibles or promissory notes, or the consignee. The "debtor" may or may not be the person who owes the obligation secured by a security interest, who is called the "obligor." § 9-102(a)(59). The "secured party" is the person who is the beneficiary of an Article 9 transaction. § 9-102(a)(72). A visualization of the definitions describing the players in the secured transaction follows:

PARTIES INVOLVED IN A SECURED TRANSACTION		
DEBTOR § 9-102(a)(28)	OBLIGOR § 9-102(a)(59)	SECURED PARTY § 9-102(a)(72)
1) PERSON HAVING INTEREST (OTHER THAN SECURITY INTEREST) IN COLLATERAL, 2) SELLER OF ACCOUNTS, CHATTEL PAPER, PAYMENT INTANGIBLES OR PROMISSORY NOTES, OR 3) CONSIGNEE	PERSON THAT 1) OWES PAYMENT OR PERFORMANCE OF SECURED OBLIGATION, 2) HAS PROVIDED PROPERTY OTHER THAN COLLATERAL TO SECURE SECURED OBLIGATION, OR 3) IS OTHERWISE ACCOUNTABLE FOR PAYMENT OR PERFORMANCE OF SECURED OBLIGATION	1) RECIPIENT OF SECURITY INTEREST, 2) PERSON HOLDING AGRICULTURAL LIEN, 3) CONSIGNOR, 4) PURCHASER OF ACCOUNTS, CHATTEL PAPER, PAYMENT INTANGIBLES OR PROMISSORY NOTES, 5) REPRESENTATIVE RECEIVING SECURITY INTEREST OR AGRICULTURAL LIEN, OR 6) PERSON HOLDING SECURITY INTEREST UNDER ART. 2, 2A, 4, 5

Section 9-203(a) tells us that a security interest "attaches" to collateral when it becomes "enforceable against the debtor" (unless the parties agree to postpone the time of attachment). The three requirements for making a security interest enforceable against the debtor are listed in § 9-203(b). A visualization of the requirements for enforceability of a security interest follows:

ENFORCEABILITY OF SECURITY INTEREST § 9-203(b)			
1) VALUE § 1-204 HAS BEEN GIVEN			
2) DEBTOR HAS RIGHTS IN THE COLLATERAL OR POWER TO TRANSFER RIGHTS			
3) SECURITY AGREEMENT § 9-102(a)(73) AND EVIDENTIARY COMPLIANCE BY ONE OF THE FOLLOWING:			
AUTHENTICATED SECURITY AGREEMENT THAT DESCRIBES COLLATERAL AND, IF TIMBER IS COVERED, DESCRIBES LAND	COLLATERAL (NOT CERTIFICATED SECURITY) IS IN POSSESSION OF SECURED PARTY PURSUANT TO SECURITY AGREEMENT	COLLATERAL IS CERTIFICATED SECURITY IN REGISTERED FORM AND IS DELIVERED TO SECURED PARTY PURSUANT TO SECURITY AGREEMENT	COLLATERAL IS DEPOSIT ACCOUNTS, ELECTRONIC CHATTEL PAPER, INVESTMENT PROPERTY OR LETTER-OF-CREDIT RIGHTS AND SECURED PARTY HAS CONTROL PURSUANT TO SECURITY AGREEMENT

The definition of "value" is in § 1-204. Although any consideration that will support a simple contract is sufficient to constitute "value," three other examples of value are provided. A visualization of the definition of "value" follows:

VALUE § 1-204			
BINDING COMMITMENT TO EXTEND CREDIT OR EXTENSION OF IMMEDIATELY AVAILABLE CREDIT	PREEXISTING CLAIM	DELIVERY UNDER PREEXISTING CONTRACT	ANY CONSIDERATION SUFFICIENT TO SUPPORT A SIMPLE CONTRACT

The extent to which the debtor has "rights in the collateral" or the "power to transfer rights in the collateral" is determined by non-Article 9 law. However, a security interest may attach to a debtor's rights in the collateral even if those rights are more limited than full ownership. Except to the extent that the priority rules provide otherwise, the rights of the secured party in the collateral are derived from those of the debtor, that is, the secured party can obtain no greater rights in the collateral than those held by the debtor prior to the grant of the security interest.

The third requirement for the enforceability of a security interest is that there is a security agreement, and adequate evidence thereof. Because Article 9 covers only consensual security interests, before a security interest may be enforceable against a debtor under Article 9, the debtor must have agreed to its creation. An "agreement that creates or provides for a security interest" is called a "security agreement." § 9-102(a)(73). An "agreement," § 1-201(b)(3), is the "bargain of the parties in fact" and may or may not be embodied in written form.

Section 9-203(b)(3) provides four ways in which evidence of a security agreement may be shown. The first is by the debtor, § 9-102(a)(28), "authenticating" a security agreement containing an adequate description of the collateral. "Authenticate" means to "sign" a written record, § 1-201(b)(37), or otherwise execute or adopt or accept a record (including an electronic record) as one's own. § 9-102(a)(7).

The authenticated security agreement must contain "a description of the collateral." Section 9-108 tells us what type of description is adequate for this purpose. Generally speaking, a description is adequate if it "reasonably identifies what is described." § 9-108(a). Section 9-108 then gives examples of descriptions that will be deemed adequate, and explicitly precludes certain other types of descriptions. A visualization of § 9-108 follows:

SUFFICIENCY OF DESCRIPTION § 9-108		
DESCRIPTION IS SUFFICIENT IF IT REASONABLY IDENTIFIES THE COLLATERAL		
DESCRIPTION IS SUFFICIENT		DESCRIPTION IS NOT SUFFICIENT
SPECIFIC LISTING		NO DESCRIPTION BY UCC TYPE FOR: 1) COMMERCIAL TORT CLAIM § 9-102(a)(13) OR 2) IN CONSUMER TRANSACTION § 9-102(a)(26) • CONSUMER GOODS • SECURITY ENTITLEMENT • SECURITIES ACCOUNT • COMMODITY ACCOUNT
CATEGORY	FOR SECURITY ENTITLEMENT, SECURITIES ACCOUNT, COMMODITY ACCOUNT, USE OF THOSE TERMS OR "INVESTMENT PROPERTY" OR DESCRIPTION OF UNDERLYING FINANCIAL ASSET OR COMMODITY CONTRACT	
UCC TYPE OF COLLATERAL		
QUANTITY		
FORMULA OR PROCEDURE		
OTHER METHOD BY WHICH COLLATERAL IS OBJECTIVELY DETERMINABLE		NO SUPERGENERIC DESCRIPTION ("ALL DEBTOR'S ASSETS" OR "ALL DEBTOR'S PERSONAL PROPERTY")

Because the other three acts that provide adequate evidence of the existence of a security agreement, pursuant to § 9-203(b)(3), are also acts that result in perfection of security interests, we will look at them further in the next chapter.

There are four situations in which the requirements of § 9-203(b) do not have to be satisfied for particular collateral because they were previously satisfied for collateral that is closely related to that collateral. In these situations described in § 9-203(f)–(i), attachment of the security interest in the related collateral automatically leads to attachment of the security interest in the collateral at issue. A visualization of these provisions for automatic attachment follows:

AUTOMATIC ATTACHMENT OF SECURITY INTEREST						
ATTACHMENT OF SECURITY INTEREST IN COLLATERAL ↑	ATTACHMENT OF SECURITY INTEREST IN "PROCEEDS" § 9-102(a)(64) AND IN A "SUPPORTING OBLIGATION" § 9-102(a)(77) § 9-203(f)	ATTACHMENT OF SECURITY INTEREST IN RIGHT TO PAYMENT OR PERFORMANCE SECURED BY SECURITY INTEREST, MORTGAGE OR LIEN ↑	ATTACHMENT OF SECURITY INTEREST IN SECURITY INTEREST, MORTGAGE OR LIEN § 9-203(g)	ATTACHMENT OF SECURITY INTEREST IN SECURITIES ACCOUNT ↑	ATTACHMENT OF SECURITY INTEREST IN SECURITY ENTITLEMENTS IN SECURITIES ACCOUNT § 9-203(h)	ATTACHMENT OF SECURITY INTEREST IN COMMODITY ACCOUNT ↑ ATTACHMENT OF SECURITY INTEREST IN COMMODITY CONTRACTS IN COMMODITY ACCOUNT § 9-203(i)

Section 9-203 provides one other situation in which compliance with § 9-203(b) is not necessary to make a security interest enforceable against a debtor. Under § 9-203(e), a security agreement entered into by one debtor (the "original debtor," § 9-102(a)(60)) may be effective to create an enforceable security interest in property of another debtor (the "new debtor," § 9-102(a)(56)) if the new debtor becomes bound as debtor under the security agreement.

There are two methods for a new debtor to become bound as debtor under the security agreement of the original debtor. The first is if, by operation of law or contract, the security interest becomes effective to create a security interest in the property of the new debtor. § 9-203(d)(1). This would occur, for example, if the new debtor expressly assumed all obligations of the original debtor under the security agreement.

Alternatively, a new debtor will become bound if, by operation of law or contract, the new debtor becomes "generally obligated for the obligations of the [original debtor] . . . and acquires or succeeds to all or substantially all of the assets of the [original debtor]." § 9-203(d)(2). This will typically occur as a result of a business reorganization, such as a change in structure from a partnership to a corporation, or from a sole proprietorship to a partnership, or as a result of a merger or acquisition of the original debtor by another entity. Although any collateral transferred from the original debtor to the new debtor in any such transformation would remain subject to a preexisting security interest, § 9-315(a)(1), if the new debtor becomes bound by the security agreement, property of the new debtor may become subject to the security interest as well.

A visualization of the provisions providing for enforceability of a security agreement against a new debtor follows:

ENFORCEABILITY OF SECURITY AGREEMENT AGAINST NEW DEBTOR

BECOMING BOUND § 9-203(d)	CONSEQUENCES § 9-203(e)
BY OPERATION OF LAW OR BY CONTRACT: SECURITY AGREEMENT BECOMES EFFECTIVE TO CREATE A SECURITY INTEREST IN NEW DEBTOR'S PROPERTY, OR NEW DEBTOR BECOMES GENERALLY OBLIGATED FOR ORIGINAL DEBTOR'S OBLIGATIONS AND ACQUIRES OR SUCCEEDS TO ALL OR SUBSTANTIALLY ALL OF ORIGINAL DEBTOR'S ASSETS	SECURITY AGREEMENT OF ORIGINAL DEBTOR IS ENFORCEABLE WITH RESPECT TO PROPERTY OF NEW DEBTOR, AND NO NEW SECURITY AGREEMENT NECESSARY

Chapter 4
PERFECTION

A security interest that has "attached" within the meaning of § 9-203 is enforceable against the debtor. A security interest that has been "perfected" as described in § 9-308 will, in most cases, be enforceable against claims of competing creditors of the debtor (including the trustee in bankruptcy if the debtor is the subject of a bankruptcy case) and persons to whom the collateral is transferred. A secured creditor always seeks to have a perfected security interest; most unperfected security interests are attributable to inadvertence or mistake.

One cannot have a perfected security interest unless the security interest has attached. This means that all three of the requirements for enforceability of a security interest described in Chapter 3 must have been satisfied. For some types of security interests, perfection occurs automatically upon attachment. For other types of security interests, perfection requires an additional step beyond those three requirements for attachment, such as possession of the collateral, control of the collateral, or filing a financing statement.

A visualization of the requirements for perfection follows:

PERFECTION § 9-308				
SECURITY INTEREST HAS ATTACHED § 9-203				
AUTOMATIC § 9-309	FILING § 9-310	COMPLIANCE WITH OTHER APPLICABLE LAW § 9-311	POSSESSION OR DELIVERY § 9-313	CONTROL § 9-314

We will now look in more detail at the various methods of perfecting security interests.

A. AUTOMATIC PERFECTION

Section 9-309 sets out 14 situations in which security interests are perfected automatically upon attachment without the need for the secured party to take any other action. A visualization of § 9-309 follows:

AUTOMATIC PERFECTION § 9-309	
1)	PURCHASE-MONEY SECURITY INTEREST § 9-103(b) IN CONSUMER GOODS
2)	ASSIGNMENT OF NOT A SIGNIFICANT PART OF ASSIGNOR'S OUTSTANDING ACCOUNTS OR PAYMENT INTANGIBLES
3)	SALE OF PAYMENT INTANGIBLE
4)	SALE OF PROMISSORY NOTE
5)	ASSIGNMENT OF HEALTH-CARE-INSURANCE RECEIVABLE § 9-102(a)(46) TO PROVIDER OF HEALTH-CARE GOODS OR SERVICES
6)	SECURITY INTEREST UNDER § 2-401, 2-505, 2-711(3) OR 2A-508(5) UNTIL DEBTOR OBTAINS POSSESSION OF COLLATERAL
7)	SECURITY INTEREST OF COLLECTING BANK UNDER § 4-210
8)	SECURITY INTEREST OF ISSUER UNDER § 5-118
9)	SECURITY INTEREST UPON DELIVERY OF FINANCIAL ASSET UNDER § 9-206(c)
10)	SECURITY INTEREST IN INVESTMENT PROPERTY CREATED BY BROKER OR SECURITIES INTERMEDIARY
11)	SECURITY INTEREST IN COMMODITY CONTRACT OR COMMODITY ACCOUNT CREATED BY COMMODITY INTERMEDIARY
12)	ASSIGNMENT FOR BENEFIT OF CREDITORS
13)	ASSIGNMENT OF BENEFICIAL INTEREST IN DECEDENT'S ESTATE
14)	SALE OF ACCOUNT THAT IS RIGHT TO PAYMENT OF LOTTERY WINNINGS

The first situation in which a security interest is automatically perfected upon attachment uses a term we have not seen before and which requires more attention, the "purchase-money security interest" (often abbreviated by commercial lawyers as "PMSI"). The PMSI in goods is defined in § 9-103(b)(1). A security interest in goods is a PMSI to the extent that the goods are "purchase-money collateral," defined in § 9-103(a)(1) as goods securing a "purchase-money obligation." "Purchase-money obligation" is defined in § 9-102(a)(2) as an obligation incurred as all or part of the purchase price of the collateral or for value given to enable the debtor to acquire rights in or use of the collateral if the value is in fact used for that purpose. One may also have a PMSI in software, as described in § 9-103(c). The definition of a PMSI in goods can be visualized as follows:

PMSI IN GOODS § 9-103(b)		
SECURITY INTEREST IN GOODS IS A PMSI TO THE EXTENT THAT:		
PURCHASE-MONEY COLLATERAL	PURCHASE-MONEY OBLIGATION	
GOODS SECURE PURCHASE-MONEY OBLIGATION INCURRED WITH RESPECT TO THOSE GOODS	OBLIGATION OF OBLIGOR IS:	
	INCURRED AS ALL OR PART OF PURCHASE PRICE OF COLLATERAL, OR	FOR VALUE GIVEN TO ENABLE DEBTOR TO ACQUIRE RIGHTS IN OR USE OF COLLATERAL IF VALUE IS IN FACT SO USED

Notice that a PMSI is always created in connection with a new acquisition of goods by the debtor. Those goods become collateral ("purchase-money collateral") for the obligation ("purchase-money obligation") to pay the purchase price of those goods to the seller, or to pay back a third party who financed the debtor's acquisition of those goods.

Courts have struggled with the problem of determining whether, and to what extent, security interests qualify as PMSIs, especially in two different cases. The first is when the obligor has made payments in respect of obligations only some of which were originally purchase-money obligations. Here the question is one of application: how should payments be allocated between purchase-money obligations and non-purchase-money obligations, and how should payments be allocated between purchase-money obligations if there is more than one?

In a transaction other than a "consumer-goods transaction" (§ 9-102(a)(24)), § 9-103(e) validates any reasonable method of application to which the parties agree. In the absence of an agreement, a payment must be applied in accordance with the intention of the obligor manifested at or before the time of payment. If the parties have no agreement, and the obligor provides no direction as to the application of the payment, § 9-103(e) directs that non-secured obligations are to be paid first, and among secured obligations, PMSIs should be paid in the order in which they were incurred (a first-in-first-out system).

The second situation in which it may be difficult to identify the extent to which a security interest constitutes a PMSI occurs when purchase-money collateral secures both a purchase-money obligation and other obligations, or when a purchase-money obligation is secured by both purchase-money collateral and other collateral, or when a purchase-money obligation is refinanced or restructured (so that the new loan is used to repay the old loan rather than to acquire the purchase-money collateral). Some courts had adopted the so-called "transformation rule" under which the PMSI was transformed into a non-purchase-money security interest when the purchase-money obligation was refinanced. Other courts concluded that the PMSI retained its character upon refinancing to the extent of the unpaid purchase-money obligation by application of the so-called "dual status rule." Still other courts would look at the facts and circumstances of each refinancing to see whether the new debt was sufficiently similar to the original purchase-money obligation that the security interest should retain its character as a PMSI.

In a transaction other than a "consumer-goods transaction," § 9-102(a)(24), § 9-103(f) explicitly adopts the dual status rule and provides that the PMSI retains its status in these situations.

In all cases other than a "consumer-goods transaction," § 9-102(a)(24), the secured party seeking to claim a PMSI has the burden of establishing the extent to which its security interests qualifies for that status. § 9-103(g).

Article 9 leaves to the court the resolution of these issues in a "consumer-goods transaction," § 9-102(a)(24), and the existence of special rules in § 9-103 dealing with these issues in non-consumer-goods transactions is intended to have no bearing on a court's decision in a consumer-goods transaction. § 9-103(h). A court may choose to adopt the same rules as for a non-consumer-goods transaction, or may adopt a different rule.

A visualization of these special rules on determining the extent to which a security interest constitutes a PMSI follows:

PROBLEM AREAS IN APPLYING DEFINITION OF PMSI IN NON-CONSUMER-GOODS TRANSACTIONS			
APPLICATION OF PAYMENTS § 9-103(e)	MIXTURE OF OBLIGATIONS AND COLLATERAL OR REFINANCING § 9-103(f)	BURDEN OF PROOF § 9-103(g)	CONSUMER-GOODS TRANSACTIONS § 9-103(h)
PAYMENTS APPLIED 1) PER REASONABLE METHOD TO WHICH PARTIES AGREE, 2) PER INTENTION OF OBLIGOR AT OR BEFORE TIME OF PAYMENT, OR 3) TO UNSECURED OBLIGATIONS BEFORE SECURED OBLIGATIONS, AND TO PMSIs IN ORDER INCURRED	PMSI RETAINS STATUS IF 1) PURCHASE-MONEY COLLATERAL SECURES NON-PURCHASE-MONEY OBLIGATION AS WELL, 2) PURCHASE-MONEY OBLIGATION IS SECURED BY NON-PURCHASE-MONEY COLLATERAL AS WELL, OR 3) PURCHASE-MONEY OBLIGATION IS RENEWED, REFINANCED, CONSOLIDATED, RESTRUCTURED	SECURED PARTY HAS BURDEN OF ESTABLISHING PMSI STATUS	COURT DETERMINES PROPER RULES IN CONSUMER-GOODS TRANSACTIONS AND RULES FOR NON-CONSUMER-GOODS TRANSACTIONS HAVE NO BEARING ON COURT

There is one other situation in which a security interest is automatically perfected upon attachment, but this automatic perfection is temporary; it expires if no other action to perfect the security interest occurs within 20 days after attachment. § 9-312(h). This temporary automatic perfection, described in § 9-312(e), applies only to security interests in certificated securities, negotiable documents, or instruments. A visualization of § 9-312(e) follows:

TEMPORARY AUTOMATIC PERFECTION
§ 9-312(e)

AUTOMATIC PERFECTION FOR 20 DAYS AFTER ATTACHMENT

1) CERTIFICATED SECURITIES, NEGOTIABLE DOCUMENTS OR INSTRUMENTS

2) TO THE EXTENT SECURITY INTEREST ARISES FOR NEW VALUE GIVEN UNDER AUTHENTICATED SECURITY AGREEMENT

B. PERFECTION BY POSSESSION OR DELIVERY

If a security interest is not automatically perfected upon attachment, the secured party must take an additional action to achieve perfection. The first action that may be available to the secured party is to take possession or delivery of the collateral. Section 9-313(a) lists those types of collateral for which perfection by taking possession or delivery of collateral is permitted; for other types of collateral, a different method of perfection must be utilized. For one type of collateral, money, perfection by taking possession is the only way of obtaining a perfected security interest. § 9-312(b)(3).

Perfection by "delivery" is used only for a certificated security. "Delivery" of a certificated security is defined in § 8-301(a) and will be discussed in connection with our examination of the concept of "control" in § 9-106.

A visualization of perfection by possession or delivery follows:

PERFECTION BY POSSESSION/DELIVERY		
PERMISSIBLE § 9-313(a)		MANDATORY § 9-312(b)
POSSESSION	DELIVERY § 8-301(a)	MONEY
TANGIBLE NEGOTIABLE DOCUMENTS GOODS INSTRUMENTS MONEY TANGIBLE CHATTEL PAPER	CERTIFICATED SECURITIES	

If goods are covered by a negotiable document and are in the possession of a bailee, a security interest in the goods may be perfected by perfecting a security interest in the document. § 9-312(c). If goods are covered by a nonnegotiable document and are in the possession of a bailee, a security interest in the goods may be perfected by issuance of a document in the name of the secured party, or the bailee's receipt of notification of the secured party's interest. § 9-312(d).

Article 9 does not define the word "possession." Instead, Official Comment 3 to § 9-313 suggests that the general principles of agency apply in determining whether a secured party has possession of collateral. Therefore, possession by an agent of the secured party is sufficient to perfect a security interest by possession. However, the debtor or someone who is solely an agent for the debtor may not act as agent for the secured party in taking possession of collateral to perfect a security interest. Similarly, Official Comment 3 states that someone who is too closely connected to or controlled by the debtor may be disqualified from serving in this role.

Section 9-313(c) provides guidance on achieving perfection by possession when the collateral (other than certificated securities and goods covered by a document) is in the possession of a third party (other than a lessee from the debtor in the ordinary course of the debtor's business) who is not acting for either the secured party or debtor. For possession by that third party to perfect the security interest of the secured party, the third party must acknowledge that it holds or will hold possession of the collateral for the secured party's benefit. The third party has no obligation to provide such an acknowledgment, § 9-313(f), and if it chooses to do so, it undertakes no duty to the secured party and need not confirm the acknowledgment to another person. § 9-313(g).

A visualization of permitted possessors of collateral for purposes of perfection by possession follows:

WHO CAN POSSESS COLLATERAL TO PERFECT SECURITY INTEREST	
PERMISSIBLE	**FORBIDDEN**
SECURED PARTY	DEBTOR
AGENT FOR SECURED PARTY AND NOT FOR DEBTOR	AGENT FOR DEBTOR AND NOT FOR SECURED PARTY
THIRD PARTY WHO ACKNOWLEDGES THAT IT HOLDS OR WILL HOLD POSSESSION FOR SECURED PARTY'S BENEFIT § 9-313(c)	THIRD PARTY "SO CLOSELY CONNECTED TO OR CONTROLLED BY THE DEBTOR" THAT DEBTOR RETAINS CONTROL

One might assume that, if possession by a secured party results in perfection, perfection terminates once possession by the secured party is relinquished. In most cases that is true, and § 9-313(d) so states. However, there are several situations in which perfection is deemed to continue despite the lack of continued possession by the secured party.

The general rule on continuation of perfection by possession and its exceptions is visualized as follows:

C. PERFECTION BY CONTROL

GENERAL RULE	CONTINUATION OF PERFECTION BY POSSESSION		EXCEPTIONS	
PERFECTION BY POSSESSION CONTINUES ONLY WHILE THE SECURED PARTY RETAINS POSSESSION § 9-313(d)	PERFECTION OF SECURITY INTEREST BY DELIVERY OF CERTIFICATED SECURITY CONTINUES UNTIL DEBTOR OBTAINS POSSESSION § 9-313(e)	SECURED PARTY WITH POSSESSION RETAINS PERFECTION UPON DELIVERY TO THIRD PARTY IF THIRD PARTY IS INSTRUCTED TO HOLD FOR SECURED PARTY OR TO REDELIVER TO SECURED PARTY § 9-313(h)	PERFECTED SECURITY INTEREST IN NEGOTIABLE DOCUMENT OR GOODS IN POSSESSION OF BAILEE CONTINUES FOR 20 DAYS IF DOCUMENTS MADE AVAILABLE TO DEBTOR FOR 1) SALE OR EXCHANGE, OR 2) LOADING, UNLOADING, STORING, SHIPPING, OR OTHER PRE-SALE DEALINGS § 9-312(f)	PERFECTED SECURITY INTEREST IN CERTIFICATED SECURITY OR INSTRUMENT CONTINUES FOR 20 DAYS IF DELIVERED TO DEBTOR FOR 1) SALE OR EXCHANGE, OR 2) PRESENTATION, COLLECTION, ENFORCEMENT, RENEWAL, OR REGISTRATION OF TRANSFER § 9-312(g)

C. PERFECTION BY CONTROL

Intangible collateral is incapable of being possessed. Therefore, for this type of collateral, Article 9 provides a second means of perfection, "control." Perfection by control is available for investment property, deposit accounts letter-of-credit rights, electronic chattel paper or electronic documents. § 9-314(a). For two of those types of collateral—deposit accounts and letter-of-credit rights—control is the exclusive means of perfecting a security interest. § 9-312(b). A visualization of the applicability of perfection by control follows:

PERFECTION BY CONTROL	
PERMISSIBLE § 9-314(a)	**MANDATORY** § 9-312(b)
INVESTMENT PROPERTY § 9-106 DEPOSIT ACCOUNTS § 9-104 LETTER-OF-CREDIT RIGHTS § 9-107 ELECTRONIC CHATTEL PAPER § 9-105 ELECTRONIC DOCUMENT § 7-106	DEPOSIT ACCOUNTS § 9-104 LETTER-OF-CREDIT RIGHTS § 9-107

For each type of collateral for which perfection by control is available, there is a separate section or sections defining how one obtains control of that type of collateral.

Investment property, § 9-102(a)(49), includes six different types of collateral and each has its own rules for obtaining control. Many of those rules are in Article 8. A visualization of perfection by control of investment property follows:

PERFECTION BY CONTROL OF INVESTMENT PROPERTY § 9-106

CERTIFICATED SECURITY § 8-106(a) & (b)	UNCERTIFICATED SECURITY § 8-106(c)	SECURITY ENTITLEMENT § 8-106(d) & (e)	COMMODITY CONTRACT § 9-106(b)	SECURITIES ACCOUNT § 9-106(c)	COMMODITY ACCOUNT § 9-106(c)
DELIVERED TO SECURED PARTY (PLUS ENDORSEMENT FOR REGISTERED FORM)	DELIVERED TO SECURED PARTY, OR ISSUER AGREES TO COMPLY WITH INSTRUCTIONS OF SECURED PARTY WITHOUT FURTHER CONSENT BY DEBTOR	SECURED CREDITOR BECOMES ENTITLEMENT HOLDER, SECURITIES INTERMEDIARY AGREES TO COMPLY WITH ORDERS OF SECURED PARTY WITHOUT FURTHER CONSENT BY DEBTOR, OR SECURED PARTY IS SECURITIES INTERMEDIARY	SECURED PARTY IS COMMODITY INTERMEDIARY, OR DEBTOR, SECURED PARTY AND COMMODITY INTERMEDIARY AGREE THAT COMMODITY INTERMEDIARY WILL COMPLY WITH ORDERS OF SECURED PARTY WITHOUT FURTHER CONSENT BY DEBTOR	CONTROL OF ALL SECURITIES ENTITLEMENTS IN SECURITIES ACCOUNT	CONTROL OF ALL COMMODITY CONTRACTS IN COMMODITY ACCOUNT

In order to understand the concept of "control" of a certificated or uncertificated security, we have to look at the definition of "delivery" in § 8-301. There are three ways of achieving delivery of a certificated security, and two ways for an uncertificated security. Although the definition uses the term "purchaser" rather than "secured party" (because it is applicable to all types of voluntary transactions creating an interest in property, including sales, leases and the like, § 1-201(b)(29) and (30)), when a secured party seeks to obtain control over a certificated or uncertificated security, the word "purchaser" in the definition of "delivery" can be read to mean "secured party." A visualization of the definition of "delivery" follows:

DELIVERY § 8-301				
CERTIFICATED SECURITY			UNCERTIFICATED SECURITY	
SECURED PARTY ACQUIRES POSSESSION OF CERTIFICATE	NON-SECURITIES INTERMEDIARY ACQUIRES POSSESSION OF CERTIFICATE ON BEHALF OF SECURED PARTY OR ACKNOWLEDGES THAT IT HOLDS FOR SECURED PARTY	SECURITIES INTERMEDIARY ACQUIRES POSSESSION OF CERTIFICATE IN REGISTERED FORM ON BEHALF OF SECURED PARTY IF CERTIFICATE IS 1) REGISTERED IN NAME OF SECURED PARTY, 2) PAYABLE TO ORDER OF SECURED PARTY, OR 3) SPECIALLY INDORSED TO SECURED PARTY	ISSUER REGISTERS SECURED PARTY AS REGISTERED OWNER	NON-SECURITIES INTERMEDIARY BECOMES REGISTERED OWNER ON BEHALF OF SECURED PARTY OR ACKNOWLEDGES THAT IT HOLDS FOR SECURED PARTY

Control of deposit accounts can be obtained in one of three ways under § 9-104. If the secured party is the bank with which the deposit account is maintained, control is automatic. If not, the secured party must either become the bank's customer with respect to the account, or must enter into a so-called "control agreement" with the bank and the debtor regarding the account. A visualization of the requirements of § 9-104 follows:

C. PERFECTION BY CONTROL 43

CONTROL OF DEPOSIT ACCOUNTS § 9-104		
SECURED PARTY IS BANK WITH WHICH DEPOSIT ACCOUNT IS MAINTAINED	DEBTOR, SECURED PARTY AND BANK AGREE THAT BANK WILL COMPLY WITH INSTRUCTIONS OF SECURED PARTY REGARDING DEPOSIT ACCOUNT WITHOUT FURTHER CONSENT OF DEBTOR	SECURED PARTY BECOMES BANK'S CUSTOMER WITH RESPECT TO DEPOSIT ACCOUNT

For letter-of-credit rights, under § 9-107 a secured party cannot obtain control without the consent of the issuer or any nominated person to the assignment of proceeds under § 5-114(c). A visualization of the requirements of § 9-107 follows:

CONTROL OF LETTER-OF-CREDIT RIGHTS § 9-107
ISSUER § 5-102(a)(9) OR NOMINATED PERSON § 5-102(a)(11) HAS CONSENTED TO AN ASSIGNMENT OF PROCEEDS OF LETTER OF CREDIT § 5-102(a)(10) UNDER § 5-114(c) OR OTHER APPLICABLE LAW OR PRACTICE

Control of electronic chattel paper is intended to be the functional equivalent of possession of tangible chattel paper. Section 9-105 describes requirements for establishing control that can be satisfied only by the development of new electronic technology. Until then, the provisions of § 9-105 are merely hortatory. A visualization of the requirements for control of electronic chattel paper follows:

CONTROL OF ELECTRONIC CHATTEL PAPER § 9-105		
SINGLE AUTHORITATIVE COPY OF RECORD OR RECORDS WHICH IS UNIQUE, IDENTIFIABLE AND UNALTERABLE EXISTS, AND ALL OF THE FOLLOWING ARE SATISFIED:		
AUTHORITATIVE COPY IDENTIFIES SECURED PARTY AS ASSIGNEE	AUTHORITATIVE COPY IS COMMUNICATED TO AND MAINTAINED BY SECURED PARTY	ANY REVISION IS READILY IDENTIFIABLE AS AUTHORIZED OR UNAUTHORIZED
	AUTHORITATIVE COPY CANNOT BE COPIED OR ASSIGNEE CHANGED WITHOUT PARTICIPATION OF SECURED PARTY	
	EACH COPY IS READILY IDENTIFIABLE AS A COPY	

Section 7-106 provides for control of electronic documents in language that closely tracks § 9-105 for electronic chattel paper. The requirements for control of electronic documents can be visualized as follows:

C. PERFECTION BY CONTROL 45

CONTROL OF ELECTRONIC DOCUMENT § 7-106			
SINGLE AUTHORITATIVE COPY OF DOCUMENT WHICH IS UNIQUE, IDENTIFIABLE AND UNALTERABLE EXISTS, AND ALL OF THE FOLLOWING ARE SATISFIED:			
AUTHORITATIVE COPY IDENTIFIES SECURED PARTY AS PERSON TO WHICH DOCUMENT WAS ISSUED OR MOST RECENTLY TRANSFERRED	AUTHORITATIVE COPY IS COMMUNICATED TO AND MAINTAINED BY SECURED PARTY	COPIES OR AMENDMENTS THAT CHANGE ASSIGNEE CAN BE MADE ONLY WITH CONSENT OF SECURED PARTY	EACH COPY IS READILY IDENTIFIABLE AS A COPY	ANY AMENDMENT IS READILY IDENTIFIABLE AS AUTHORIZED OR UNAUTHORIZED

As was true for perfection by possession, the general rule is that perfection by control continues only so long as control is maintained. § 9-314(b). However, for investment property, perfection may continue in some cases even after the secured party no longer has control. A visualization of the continuation of perfection by control follows:

CONTINUATION OF PERFECTION BY CONTROL	
GENERAL RULE	**EXCEPTION**
PERFECTION BY CONTROL CONTINUES ONLY WHILE THE SECURED PARTY RETAINS CONTROL § 9-314(b)	SECURITY INTEREST IN INVESTMENT PROPERTY REMAINS PERFECTED BY CONTROL UNTIL SECURED PARTY DOES NOT HAVE CONTROL AND 1) FOR CERTIFICATED SECURITY, DEBTOR HAS POSSESSION OF CERTIFICATE, 2) FOR UNCERTIFICATED SECURITY, ISSUER HAS REGISTERED DEBTOR AS REGISTERED OWNER, OR 3) FOR SECURITY ENTITLEMENT, THE DEBTOR IS THE ENTITLEMENT HOLDER

D. PERFECTION BY COMPLIANCE WITH OTHER LAW

A third way in which a secured party may perfect its security interest if that interest is not automatically perfected upon attachment is to comply with non-Article 9 law when that is applicable to the transaction. There are three situations in which a law other than Article 9 might apply to the perfection of security interests in personal property. The first is when federal law has preempted Article 9. The second is when the personal property is the type for which the state has adopted a certificate of title statute. The third is when the property is covered by a certificate of title statute of another jurisdiction. These situations are described in § 9-311. A visualization of § 9-311 follows:

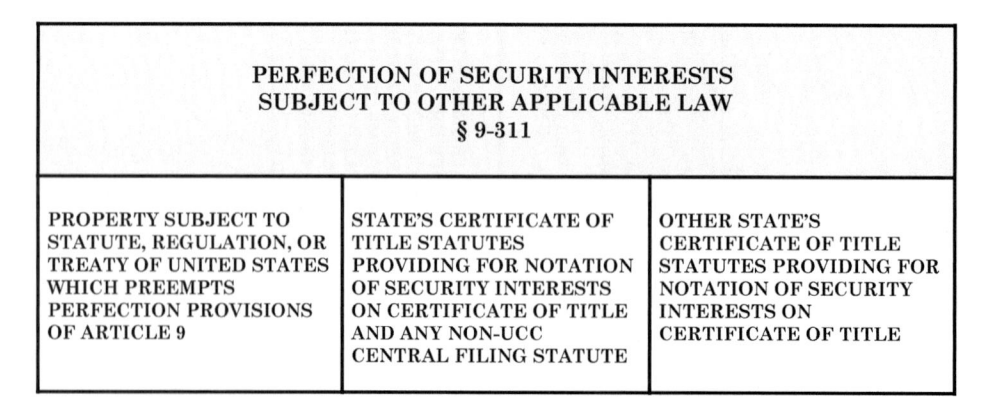

PERFECTION OF SECURITY INTERESTS SUBJECT TO OTHER APPLICABLE LAW § 9-311		
PROPERTY SUBJECT TO STATUTE, REGULATION, OR TREATY OF UNITED STATES WHICH PREEMPTS PERFECTION PROVISIONS OF ARTICLE 9	STATE'S CERTIFICATE OF TITLE STATUTES PROVIDING FOR NOTATION OF SECURITY INTERESTS ON CERTIFICATE OF TITLE AND ANY NON-UCC CENTRAL FILING STATUTE	OTHER STATE'S CERTIFICATE OF TITLE STATUTES PROVIDING FOR NOTATION OF SECURITY INTERESTS ON CERTIFICATE OF TITLE

E. PERFECTION BY FILING

In the case of those security interests for which Article 9 does not state that the exclusive means for perfection is possession or control, the secured party may perfect its security interest by filing. In the case of those security interests for which another means of perfection is not explicitly authorized, perfection by filing is the only permissible method. A visualization of § 9-310 on perfection by filing follows:

PERFECTION BY FILING § 9-310	
GENERAL RULE	EXCEPTIONS
FINANCING STATEMENT MUST BE FILED TO PERFECT SECURITY INTEREST	1) PERFECTION OF SECURITY INTERESTS IN COLLATERAL RELATED TO COLLATERAL AS TO WHICH PERFECTION OCCURS § 9-308(d)-(g) 2) PERFECTION UPON ATTACHMENT § 9-309 3) PROPERTY WHOSE PERFECTION IS GOVERNED BY OTHER APPLICABLE LAW § 9-311 4) GOODS IN THE POSSESSION OF BAILEE COVERED BY A NON-NEGOTIABLE DOCUMENT § 9-312(d) 5) TEMPORARY PERFECTION § 9-312(e)-(g) 6) PERFECTION BY POSSESSION § 9-313 7) PERFECTION OF CERTIFICATED SECURITY BY DELIVERY § 9-313 8) PERFECTION BY CONTROL § 9-314 9) PERFECTION IN PROCEEDS § 9-315 10) PERFECTION UPON A CHANGE IN GOVERNING LAW § 9-316

The Article 9 provisions relating to filings are grouped in Part 5 of that Article. We are going to look at four issues:

(1) What do you file?

(2) Who is permitted to file?

(3) What does it mean to "file"?

(4) Where do you file?

1. What Do You File?

Section 9-310(a) requires that a "financing statement," § 9-102(a)(39), be filed to perfect a security interest. The requirements for this financing statement are minimal. Section 9-502 requires that a financing statement contain only three things to be sufficient, unless the collateral covers as-extracted collateral or timber to be cut, or is filed as a fixture filing with respect to goods that are to become fixtures. A visualization of the requirements of § 9-502 follows:

REQUIREMENTS FOR FINANCING STATEMENT § 9-502	
FOR ALL COLLATERAL	FOR AS-EXTRACTED COLLATERAL OR TIMBER TO BE CUT OR FIXTURE FILINGS COVERING GOODS TO BECOME FIXTURES
1) NAME OF DEBTOR 2) NAME OF SECURED PARTY OR ITS REPRESENTATIVE 3) INDICATES COLLATERAL COVERED	1) INDICATES THAT IT COVERS THIS TYPE OF COLLATERAL, 2) INDICATES THAT IT IS TO BE FILED IN REAL ESTATE RECORDS, 3) PROVIDES DESCRIPTION OF REAL PROPERTY TO WHICH COLLATERAL IS RELATED, AND 4) IF DEBTOR DOES NOT HAVE INTEREST OF RECORD IN REAL PROPERTY, PROVIDES NAME OF RECORD OWNER

Although a financing statement that includes only the elements required by § 9-502 is effective upon filing, the filing office may refuse to accept an initial financing statement if it does not include the information required by § 9-516(b), and the filing office is directed to do so, § 9-520(a). A visualization of these additional requirements follows:

ADDITIONAL REQUIREMENTS FOR FINANCING STATEMENT TO AVOID REFUSAL BY FILING OFFICE § 9-516(b)	
INFORMATION ON SECURED PARTY § 9-516(b)(4)	INFORMATION ON DEBTOR § 9-516(b)(5)
NAME AND MAILING ADDRESS OF SECURED PARTY	MAILING ADDRESS OF DEBTOR INDICATION WHETHER DEBTOR IS INDIVIDUAL OR ORGANIZATION IF DEBTOR IS ORGANIZATION, 1) TYPE OF ORGANIZATION, 2) JURISDICTION OF ORGANIZATION, OR 3) ORGANIZATIONAL IDENTIFICATION NUMBER

If a filed financing statement includes the information about the debtor described in § 9-516(b)(5), but that information is incorrect at the time the financing statement is filed, the financing statement remains effective. However, the security interest may not prevail against certain competing parties who are misled by the erroneous information. Section 9-338, which protects these competing secured creditors and other purchasers, can be visualized as follows:

FINANCING STATEMENT WITH ERRONEOUS DEBTOR INFORMATION § 9-338			
RULE	EXCEPTIONS			
FILED FINANCING STATEMENT WITH INFORMATION REQUIRED BY § 9-516(b)(5) WHICH IS INCORRECT AT TIME OF FILING IS EFFECTIVE	CONFLICTING PERFECTED SECURITY INTEREST PREVAILS IF HOLDER GIVES VALUE IN REASONABLE RELIANCE UPON INCORRECT INFORMATION	PURCHASER OTHER THAN SECURED PARTY TAKES COLLATERAL FREE OF SECURITY INTEREST TO EXTENT THAT PURCHASER IN REASONABLE RELIANCE GIVES VALUE AND, IN CASE OF TANGIBLE CHATTEL PAPER, TANGIBLE DOCUMENTS, GOODS, INSTRUMENTS OR A SECURITY CERTIFICATE, TAKES DELIVERY

Section 9-521(a) provides a uniform version of an initial financing statement that includes all the required information to make it effective and to ensure that the filing office will not decline to accept it for filing.

The first requirement for a financing statement is that it provide the name of the debtor. Section 9-503(a) tells us how to determine what name to use for this purpose. There are different rules depending on whether the debtor is a "registered organization," § 9-102(a)(70) (meaning an organization organized under the law of a state or the United States as to which that jurisdiction must maintain a public record of its organization), a decedent's estate, a trust or trustee, or another type of debtor. A visualization of the requirements of § 9-503(a) follows:

SUFFICIENCY OF DEBTOR'S NAME § 9-503(a)				
REGISTERED ORGANIZATION § 9-102(a)(70)	DECEDENT'S ESTATE	TRUST OR TRUSTEE FOR PROPERTY HELD IN TRUST	OTHER DEBTOR	
			WITH A NAME:	WITHOUT A NAME:
NAME ON PUBLIC RECORDS OF JURISDICTION OF ORGANIZATION	NAME OF DECEDENT AND INDICATION THAT DEBTOR IS ESTATE	NAME OF TRUST ON DOCUMENTS OF CREATION OR NAME OF SETTLOR AND IDENTIFICATION OF TRUST AND INDICATION THAT DEBTOR IS TRUST OR TRUSTEE	INDIVIDUAL OR ORGANIZATION NAME	NAMES OF PARTNERS, MEMBERS, ASSOCIATES, CONSTITUENTS

Although a secured party may include additional information about the debtor, such as a trade name, inclusion of that information does not render the financing statement ineffective, § 9-503(b), but use of a trade name alone is not sufficient. § 9-503(c). A financing statement may include the name of more than one debtor. § 9-503(e).

As to the name of the secured party, § 9-503 tells us only that there may be more than one secured party listed, § 9-503(e), and that failure to disclose the representative capacity of a secured party does not render the financing statement insufficient. § 9-503(d).

A financing statement must also indicate the collateral that is covered by it. Section 9-504 provides direction on how one describes collateral in a way that satisfies this requirement. It permits either the type of description that was adequate for purposes of the security agreement (visualized in the last chapter), or a super-generic description, such as "all assets" or "all personal property." A visualization of the requirements of § 9-504 follows:

SUFFICIENCY OF COLLATERAL DESCRIPTION § 9-504	
DESCRIPTION OF COLLATERAL PURSUANT TO § 9-108	INDICATION THAT FINANCING STATEMENT COVERS ALL ASSETS OR ALL PERSONAL PROPERTY

Despite the fact that the requirements are easy to satisfy, § 9-506(a) nevertheless provides that minor errors or omissions in a financing statement that substantially complies with the filing requirements of Article 9 do not render it ineffective unless they make the financing statement "seriously misleading." As a general rule, a mistake in the name of the debtor (that is, failure to comply with the requirements of § 9-503) renders a financing statement seriously misleading, unless a search of the filing records under the debtor's correct name (determined in accordance with § 9-503) using the filing office's standard search logic would disclose the filing. A mistake in the name of the secured party should never be seriously misleading, because that name is not used to index the filing. Whether a mistake in the description of the collateral is seriously misleading would be an issue for determination by a court. A visualization of the substantial compliance doctrine of § 9-506 follows:

SUBSTANTIAL COMPLIANCE DOCTRINE § 9-506			
FINANCING STATEMENT IS EFFECTIVE, DESPITE MINOR ERRORS OR OMISSIONS, UNLESS SERIOUSLY MISLEADING § 9-506(a)			
DEBTOR'S NAME		SECURED PARTY'S NAME	INDICATION OF COLLATERAL
RULE § 9-506(b)	EXCEPTION § 9-506(c)	ERROR IS NEVER SERIOUSLY MISLEADING – OFFICIAL COMMENT 2 TO § 9-506	COURT DECIDES WHETHER ERROR IS SERIOUSLY MISLEADING
FINANCING STATEMENT WITHOUT NAME COMPLYING WITH § 9-503(a) IS SERIOUSLY MISLEADING	IF SEARCH OF RECORDS UNDER DEBTOR'S § 9-503(a) NAME USING STANDARD SEARCH LOGIC OF FILING OFFICE WOULD DISCLOSE FINANCING STATEMENT, IT IS NOT SERIOUSLY MISLEADING		

Even if a financing statement is not seriously misleading at the time it is filed and is therefore effective at that time to provide notice of a possible security interest to those who search for it, facts may change after filing that make the financing statement inaccurate and unable to accomplish its purpose. Recall that pursuant to § 9-502, the only required elements of a financing statement in most cases are the name of the debtor, the name of the secured party or its representative, and a description of the collateral. Therefore, the type of post-filing change that would impact a financing statement would be a change in the name or identity of the debtor, a change in the name or identity of the secured party, or a change in the collateral.

Section 9-507 addresses the issue of post-filing events that bear on the effectiveness of the financing statement. The general rule provided in § 9-507(b) is that a financing statement does not become ineffective by reason of post-filing changes, even if they render the financing statement seriously misleading. However, there are two exceptions. The first is when the debtor changes its name. The second is when the debtor is a different entity than the original debtor.

The name of the debtor can change after an initial financing statement is filed by reason of a voluntary selection of a new name. For example, a debtor may get married and assume the spouse's last name or select a new name that combines the names of the two parties, or a corporate debtor may decide to change its name for market reasons (such as from Philip Morris Companies,

Inc. to Altria Group, Inc.). In this situation, § 9-507(c) tells us that if the change in the name renders the financing statement "seriously misleading" (meaning, per § 9-506, that a search of the filing office records under the debtor's new correct name using the filing office's standard search logic will not disclose the original filing), the original (now seriously misleading) filing remains effective with respect to collateral acquired by the debtor before or within four months after the name change, but is ineffective with respect to collateral acquired by the debtor more than four months after the name change unless it is amended to reflect the new name.

A visualization of the rule on post-filing changes follows:

POST-FILING CHANGES § 9-507		
RULE	**EXCEPTION**	
A FINANCING STATEMENT IS NOT RENDERED INEFFECTIVE IF POST-FILING CHANGE MAKES IT SERIOUSLY MISLEADING	DEBTOR CHANGES NAME TO ONE THAT MAKES FINANCING STATEMENT SERIOUSLY MISLEADING	
	FILING EFFECTIVE AS TO COLLATERAL ACQUIRED BEFORE OR WITHIN FOUR MONTHS AFTER CHANGE	FILING NOT EFFECTIVE AS TO COLLATERAL ACQUIRED MORE THAN FOUR MONTHS AFTER CHANGE

The identity of the debtor can change in two ways. The first is by the transfer of the collateral from the original debtor to another entity. Because the definition of "debtor" in § 9-102(a)(28) includes any person "having an interest . . . in the collateral," if the collateral is "sold, leased, licensed, or otherwise disposed of," § 9-507(a) states that the filed financing statement remains effective with respect to that collateral, even if a search under the name of the new possessor of the collateral would not disclose the filing.

The second situation in which the identity of the debtor may change is through a change in the legal organization of the debtor. For example, the debtor, an individual, may decide to incorporate his or her business or may enter into a partnership with another person, or a corporate debtor may merge into another corporation. As we saw in Chapter 3, a new debtor may become bound by a security agreement of an original debtor under the circumstances described in § 9-203(d) and (e). But if the name of the new debtor differs significantly from the name of the original debtor, the financing statement may become seriously misleading. Therefore, § 9-508 employs the same approach as § 9-507(c) by making the original financing statement effective with respect to collateral acquired by the new debtor before and within four months after the new debtor become bound by the original security agreement, but ineffective with respect to collateral acquired by the new debtor more than four months after that time unless an initial financing statement providing the name of the new debtor is filed prior to that time.

A visualization of the rules with respect to a change in the identity of the debtor follows:

POST-FILING NEW DEBTOR § 9-508		
RULE	EXCEPTION	
A FINANCING STATEMENT NAMING ORIGINAL DEBTOR IS EFFECTIVE WITH RESPECT TO COLLATERAL IN WHICH NEW DEBTOR HAS INTEREST	NAME OF NEW DEBTOR MAKES FINANCING STATEMENT SERIOUSLY MISLEADING	
	FILING EFFECTIVE AS TO COLLATERAL ACQUIRED BY NEW DEBTOR BEFORE OR WITHIN FOUR MONTHS AFTER NEW DEBTOR BECOMES BOUND UNDER § 9-203(d)	FILING NOT EFFECTIVE AS TO COLLATERAL ACQUIRED MORE THAN FOUR MONTHS AFTER NEW DEBTOR BECOMES BOUND UNDER § 9-203(d)

The "financing statement" is composed of the initial financing statement and any filed record relating to the initial financing statement. § 9-102(a)(39). There are several different types of record that may be filed after the initial financing statement and we should look at what they accomplish.

The first additional type of filing discussed in Part 5 of Article 9 is the amendment, described in § 9-512. As the name suggests, the purpose of an amendment is to amend the information contained in the financing statement then on file. A standard form of amendment is provided in § 9-521(b). A visualization of the provisions relating to an amendment follows:

AMENDMENT § 9-512		
DEFINITION	EFFECT	EXCEPTIONS
1) IDENTIFIES INITIAL FINANCING STATEMENT BY FILE NUMBER 2) IF INITIAL FINANCING STATEMENT RELATES TO AS-EXTRACTED COLLATERAL OR TIMBER TO BE CUT OR FIXTURES, CONTAINS § 9-502(b) INFORMATION	ADD OR DELETE COLLATERAL, CONTINUE OR TERMINATE EFFECTIVENESS OF FINANCING STATEMENT, OR AMEND INFORMATION CONTAINED IN FINANCING STATEMENT	CANNOT DELETE ALL DEBTORS CANNOT DELETE ALL SECURED PARTIES

The second type of additional filing is the termination statement, defined in § 9-102(a)(79). The purpose of a termination statement (which is a form of amendment) is to terminate the effectiveness of a filed financing statement. If no such termination statement is filed, a financing statement generally remains effective for a period of five years, § 9-515 (discussed in connection with continuation statements). Pursuant to § 9-513, the secured party always has an obligation to file a termination statement within 20 days after receiving an authenticated request by the debtor or if the filing of the financing statement was not authorized. In addition, if the financing statement covers consumer goods, the secured party must file a termination statement within one month after the secured transaction terminates even if the debtor has not made a request. A visualization of the provisions dealing with termination statements follows:

TERMINATION STATEMENT
§ 9-513

DEFINITION § 9-102(a)(79)	EFFECT	WHEN MUST IT BE FILED	
		CREDIT SECURED BY CONSUMER GOODS:	CREDIT NOT SECURED BY CONSUMER GOODS:
1) IDENTIFIES INITIAL FINANCING STATEMENT BY FILE NUMBER	TERMINATES EFFECTIVENESS OF FINANCING STATEMENT	WITHIN ONE MONTH (OR, IF EARLIER, WITHIN 20 DAYS AFTER REQUEST BY DEBTOR) AFTER END OF CREDIT OR IF FILING WAS NOT AUTHORIZED	WITHIN 20 DAYS AFTER REQUEST BY DEBTOR AFTER END OF CREDIT OR IF FILING WAS NOT AUTHORIZED
2) INDICATES THAT IT IS TERMINATION STATEMENT OR THAT FINANCING STATEMENT IS NO LONGER TO BE EFFECTIVE			

The assignment is another form of amendment, and is intended to reflect a transfer of the secured party's power to authorize an amendment to a financing statement, making the transferee the new secured party of record under § 9-511. An assignment may be made in any of three ways: on the initial financing statement, by an amendment to the financing statement, or (in the case of fixtures) by the assignment of a mortgage effective as a fixture filing. Assignment of the secured party's powers is not necessary to make the assignment valid as against creditors of and transferees from the debtor, § 9-310(c), but if the assignment is itself part of a transaction within the scope of Article 9, a filing is necessary to make it effective against creditors of and transferees from the original secured creditor. Official Comment 4 to § 9-310.

A visualization of the assignment provisions follows:

ASSIGNMENT § 9-514

PURPOSE	METHODS OF ASSIGNING		RESULT	NOT REQUIRED
TO ASSIGN OF RECORD ALL OR PART OF SECURED PARTY'S POWER TO AUTHORIZE AN AMENDMENT TO A FINANCING STATEMENT	REFLECT ASSIGNMENT ON INITIAL FINANCING STATEMENT	AMENDMENT TO FINANCING STATEMENT WHICH 1) IDENTIFIES INITIAL FINANCING STATEMENT BY FILE NUMBER, 2) PROVIDES NAME OF ASSIGNOR, AND 3) PROVIDES NAME AND MAILING ADDRESS OF ASSIGNEE	ASSIGNEE BECOMES SECURED PARTY OF RECORD § 9-511	TO MAKE ASSIGNMENT EFFECTIVE AGAINST CREDITORS OF AND TRANSFEREES FROM DEBTOR
		ASSIGNMENT OF MORTGAGE EFFECTIVE AS FIXTURE FILING		

The continuation statement is yet another form of amendment designed to continue the effectiveness of the financing statement beyond its then-applicable duration. In most cases, a financing statement remains effective for a period of five years after the date of filing. § 9-515(a). However, the period is 30 years for a "public-finance transaction," § 9-102(a)(67) (a secured transaction in which a state or governmental unit thereof is involved also involving the issuance of long-term debt securities) or a "manufactured-home transaction," § 9-102(a)(54) (a secured transaction creating a PMSI in a "manufactured home," § 9-102(a)(53), or in which a manufactured home is the primary collateral). § 9-515(b). A financing statement filed with respect to a debtor who is a "transmitting utility," § 9-102(a)(80), is effective until terminated. § 9-515(f). In addition, if a mortgage is effective as a fixture filing, it remains effective until the mortgage is released or satisfied or otherwise terminates. § 9-515(g).

A continuation statement may be filed only within six months before the expiration of the effectiveness of the filed financing statement, § 9-515(d). The filing office is authorized (and required) to reject a continuation statement that is presented for filing outside that six-month window, § 9-516(b)(7) and § 9-520(a), and if it is accepted for filing, it is ineffective. § 9-510(c).

An effective financing statement continues the effectiveness of the initial financing statement for an additional five years beyond the day on which it would otherwise have become ineffective, and each successive continuation statement continues the effectiveness of the financing statement for an additional five-year period. § 9-515(e).

When a financing statement lapses, it is no longer effective to perfect a security interest and, if the security interest becomes unperfected as a result (because no other action to perfect it has been taken prior to the lapse), it is deemed never to have been perfected as against a "purchaser" of the collateral for value. § 9-515(c). A "purchaser" (defined in § 1-201(b)(30) as one who takes by "purchase" within the meaning of § 1-201(b)(29)) would include, among others, a secured creditor whose interest arose prior to the lapse.

A visualization of the provisions dealing with the duration and effectiveness of financing statements follows:

DURATION AND EFFECTIVENESS OF FINANCING STATEMENT § 9-515					
DEFINITION OF CONTINUATION STATEMENT	EFFECT OF CONTINUATION STATEMENT	DURATION OF FINANCING STATEMENT		EFFECT OF LAPSE	TIMING
^	^	GENERAL RULE	EXCEPTIONS § 9-515(b), (f) & (g)	^	^
§ 9-102(a)(27) 1) IDENTIFIES INITIAL FINANCING STATEMENT BY FILE NUMBER 2) INDICATES THAT IT IS A CONTINUATION STATEMENT FOR THAT FINANCING STATEMENT OR THAT EFFECTIVENESS OF FINANCING STATEMENT IS TO BE CONTINUED	CONTINUES EFFECTIVENESS OF FINANCING STATEMENT FOR ADDITIONAL FIVE YEAR TERM FROM END OF INITIAL TERM (OR END OF PREVIOUSLY-EXTENDED TERM) § 9-515(e)	FIVE YEARS AFTER DATE OF FILING § 9-515(a)	PUBLIC-FINANCE TRANSACTION § 9-102(a)(67) (30 YEARS) MANUFACTURED-HOME TRANSACTION § 9-102(a)(54) (30 YEARS) TRANSMITTING UTILITY § 9-102(a)(80) (NO LIMIT) MORTGAGE AS FIXTURE FILING (UNTIL MORTGAGE TERMINATES)	FINANCING STATEMENT CEASES TO PERFECT SECURITY INTEREST, AND SECURITY INTEREST IS DEEMED NEVER TO HAVE BEEN PERFECTED AS AGAINST A PURCHASER FOR VALUE § 9-515(c)	MAY BE FILED ONLY WITHIN SIX MONTHS BEFORE EXPIRATION OF TERM § 9-515(d) UNTIMELY FILING INEFFECTIVE § 9-510(c)

The final type of filing described in Part 5 of Article 9 is the correction statement. The correction statement has no legal effect, § 9-518(c), but allows a person who believes that a filed record is inaccurate or was wrongfully filed to place that belief in the public record. A visualization of the provisions relating to the correction statement follows:

CORRECTION STATEMENT § 9-518	
CONTENTS	EFFECT
1) IDENTIFIES RECORD TO WHICH IT RELATES BY FILE NUMBER 2) INDICATES THAT IT IS A CORRECTION STATEMENT 3) PROVIDES BASIS FOR BELIEF THAT RECORD IS INACCURATE AND HOW IT SHOULD BE AMENDED TO BE ACCURATE, OR BASIS FOR BELIEF THAT RECORD WAS WRONGFULLY FILED	DOES NOT AFFECT EFFECTIVENESS OF FILED RECORD

2. Who Is Permitted to File?

A record may be filed only if the appropriate party authorizes the filing of that record. Section 9-509 specifies who is the appropriate party to authorize different types of records. For the initial financing statement and any amendment that adds collateral or adds a debtor, the debtor must authorize the filing. For any other amendment to a financing statement, the secured party of record must generally authorize the filing. However, if the amendment is a termination statement which the secured party was required to file under § 9-513(b) or (c) and the secured party fails to file, the debtor is authorized to make the filing itself. If a filing is made without authorization by the appropriate party, it is not effective. § 9-510(a). A visualization of § 9-509 follows:

AUTHORIZATION OF FILING § 9-509		
WHO MAY AUTHORIZE FILING		FORM OF AUTHORIZATION
DEBTOR	SECURED PARTY OF RECORD	1) SEPARATE DOCUMENT, 2) SECURITY AGREEMENT AS TO FILING FINANCING STATEMENT COVERING COLLATERAL DESCRIBED THEREIN AND PROCEEDS, OR 3) ACQUISITION OF COLLATERAL SUBJECT TO SECURITY INTEREST AS TO FILING FINANCING STATEMENT FOR SUCH COLLATERAL AND PROCEEDS
INITIAL FINANCING STATEMENT, AMENDMENT ADDING COLLATERAL OR ADDING DEBTOR TERMINATION STATEMENT IF SECURED PARTY OF RECORD IS REQUIRED TO FILE UNDER § 9-503(a) OR (c) AND HAS NOT DONE SO	ANY OTHER AMENDMENT	

3. What Does It Mean to File?

The acts that have the legal consequence of "filing" a record are described in § 9-516(a). There are three different acts that constitute "filing." The first is communication of a record to the filing office and tender of the filing fee. To "communicate" a record means to send it in tangible form, transmit it by any other means agreed between the sender and recipient, or (in the case of a record communicated to a filing office) transmitting it by any means prescribed by a rule adopted by the filing office. § 9-102(a)(18). A second act that constitutes "filing" is the acceptance of the record by the filing office (even if that acceptance is not accompanied by the filing fee). The final act that constitutes "filing" is rejection of the record by the filing office after that record has been communicating to the filing office with tender of the filing fee if the rejection is for an improper reason. The only proper reasons for rejecting a record are set out in § 9-516(b). Although improperly rejected records will be deemed "filed," such filings are not effective against a "purchaser" of the collateral, § 1-201(b)(30), which gives value in reasonable reliance upon the absence of the record from the files. § 9-516(d).

If a record is properly filed within the meaning of § 9-516, the failure of the filing office to index it properly does not render it ineffective even though it will not be found by a subsequent search. § 9-517.

A visualization of the provisions of § 9-516 follows:

MECHANICS OF FILING § 9-516			
ACTS CONSTITUTING FILING			GROUNDS FOR REFUSAL TO ACCEPT RECORD § 9-516(b)
COMMUNICATION § 9-102(a)(18) OF RECORD TO FILING OFFICE + TENDER OF FILING FEE	ACCEPTANCE OF RECORD BY FILING OFFICE	COMMUNICATION § 9-102(a)(18) OF RECORD TO FILING OFFICE + TENDER OF FILING FEE + REFUSAL OF FILING OFFICE TO ACCEPT RECORD FOR REASON OTHER THAN § 9-516(b) GROUNDS EXCEPTION: FILING NOT EFFECTIVE AGAINST PURCHASER § 1-201(b)(30) OF COLLATERAL WHO GIVES VALUE IN REASONABLE RELIANCE ON ABSENCE OF FILED RECORD	1) RECORD NOT COMMUNICATED BY AUTHORIZED METHOD 2) APPLICABLE FILING FEE NOT TENDERED 3) FILING OFFICE CANNOT INDEX BECAUSE OF INADEQUATE INFORMATION 4) NO NAME AND MAILING ADDRESS FOR SECURED PARTY OF RECORD 5) MISSING INFORMATION ABOUT DEBTOR 6) MISSING INFORMATION ABOUT ASSIGNEE FOR ASSIGNMENT 7) UNTIMELY CONTINUATION STATEMENT

4. Where Do You File?

If a particular state's law is applicable with respect to perfection of a security interest or agricultural lien, the place of filing within that state under § 9-501 depends on the type of collateral involved. If the collateral is real-estate related (as-extracted collateral, § 9-102(a)(6), timber to the cut, or fixtures, § 9-102(a)(41), and the filing is made as a fixture filing), the place of filing is the place one would file a mortgage on the real property to which the collateral is related. In all other cases, the state may specify a single central office for filings. If the state wishes, it may designate a different office for filings against collateral of a transmitting utility, § 9-102(a)(80).

A visualization of § 9-501 specifying the applicable filing office follows:

PLACE OF FILING § 9-501		
GENERAL RULE FOR MOST COLLATERAL	AS-EXTRACTED COLLATERAL (§ 9-102(a)(6)), TIMBER TO BE CUT, FIXTURE FILINGS	COLLATERAL OF TRANSMITTING UTILITY (§ 9-102(a)(80))
CENTRAL FILING	REAL ESTATE RECORDS	AS SPECIFIED BY STATE IN STATUTE

Chapter 5
CHOICE OF LAW

Generally speaking, parties engaging in a commercial transaction have the power to choose the law to govern their rights and obligations. So long as the parties are not consumers, an agreement by parties to a "domestic transaction" (one lacking a reasonable relationship to a country other than the United States, § 1-301(a)(1)) may agree to an applicable state law whether or not the transaction bears a relation to the designated state. § 1-301(c)(1). If one of the parties is a consumer, the parties may select the law of any state if the transaction bears a reasonable relation to the state designated. § 1-301(e)(1).

However, as § 1-301(g)(8) indicates, Article 9 contains mandatory choice of law rules that render a contrary agreement by the parties ineffective. Although the parties to a secured transaction may select the state law that governs attachment, validity, characterization and enforcement of their security interest, the issues of perfection, the effect of perfection or nonperfection, and the priority of a security interest implicate the rights of parties other than the debtor and the secured party and should not be subject to bilateral agreement. For example, a third party must be able to determine (without examining the debtor's contracts) in which state's records a search should be conducted to find a filed financing statement against the debtor.

The choice of law provisions with respect to perfection, the effect of perfection or nonperfection and priority of security interests are contained in Subpart 1 of Part 3 of Article 9, §§ 9-301 through 9-307. The basic rule is contained in § 9-301(1). It tells us that while a debtor is located in a jurisdiction, the local law of that jurisdiction governs perfection, the effect of perfection and nonperfection and priority of a security interest. (There is a separate choice of law rule for agricultural liens on farm products in § 9-302 designating the law of the jurisdiction in which the farm products are located.)

Application of this general rule obviously requires that we understand where the "location" of the debtor is. Section 9-307 addresses this issue. A debtor's location depends on the nature of the debtor. If the debtor is an individual, the debtor is located at the individual's principal residence. If the debtor is an organization, the rule looks at the type of organization. A "registered organization," § 9-102(a)(70) (one organized solely under the laws of a single state or the United States as to which there is a public record showing its organization) organized under the laws of a state is located in that state. Other organizations are located at their place of business if they have only one, and their chief executive office if they have more than one place of business. There are also special rules for the United States as a debtor, for "registered organizations" organized under the laws of the United States, for foreign bank branches or agencies, and for foreign air carriers.

A visualization of the rules on location of the debtor follows:

LOCATION OF DEBTOR § 9-307

INDIVIDUAL	ORGANIZATION			UNITED STATES	FOREIGN BANK BRANCHES AND AGENCIES		FOREIGN AIR CARRIERS
	REGISTERED		OTHER				
	UNDER STATE LAW	UNDER U.S. LAW			LICENSED IN ONE STATE	LICENSED IN MORE THAN ONE STATE	
PRINCIPAL RESIDENCE	JURISDICTION OF REGISTRATION	IF U.S. LAW DESIGNATES A STATE, THAT STATE; IF U.S. LAW AUTHORIZES DEBTOR TO DESIGNATE A STATE, THAT STATE; OTHERWISE, DISTRICT OF COLUMBIA	IF ONLY ONE PLACE OF BUSINESS, THAT PLACE OF BUSINESS; IF MORE THAN ONE PLACE OF BUSINESS, CHIEF EXECUTIVE OFFICE	DISTRICT OF COLUMBIA	STATE IN WHICH LICENSED	IF U.S. LAW DESIGNATES A STATE, THAT STATE; IF U.S. LAW AUTHORIZES DEBTOR TO DESIGNATE A STATE, THAT STATE; OTHERWISE, DISTRICT OF COLUMBIA	DESIGNATED OFFICE FOR SERVICE OF PROCESS

A registered organization continues to be located in the applicable jurisdiction even if its status as a registered organization or its existence terminates. § 9-307(g). Similarly, an individual or organization other than a registered organization continues to be located in the applicable jurisdiction even if he, she or it ceases to exist, have a residence, or have a place of business. § 9-307(d).

Although the location of the debtor is the general rule with respect to choice of law for Article 9, there are seven situations in which another choice of law rule is provided. The first is for possessory security interests. Under § 9-301(2), the perfection, effect of perfection or nonperfection and priority of such possessory security interests is determined by the law of the jurisdiction in which the collateral is located.

The second involves collateral that is intimately related to real property—security interests in fixtures perfected by a fixture filing, security interests in timber to be cut, and security interests in as-extracted collateral. For fixtures and timber to be cut, the law of the jurisdiction in which the collateral is located governs. § 9-301(3). For as-extracted collateral, the law of the jurisdiction in which the wellhead or minehead is located governs. § 9-301(4).

The third relates to tangible collateral—tangible negotiable documents, goods, instruments, money, or tangible chattel paper. Because a secured creditor would have to execute upon its tangible collateral in the jurisdiction in which the collateral is located, § 9-301(3)(C) makes that law applicable to the effect of perfection or nonperfection and priority of a security interest in that collateral. The law of the jurisdiction in which the collateral is located does *NOT* govern perfection of the security interest. Thus, if the debtor has inventory in Illinois but is a Delaware corporation, perfection would be governed by the law of Delaware (and a secured creditor would make a filing to perfect its security interest in Delaware), but Illinois law would govern the effect of perfection or nonperfection and priority of the security interest when the inventory is seized and sold.

The fourth exception applies to goods covered by a "certificate of title," § 9-102(a)(10), on which security interests are noted. When goods are covered by a certificate of title, the law of the jurisdiction under whose certificate of title the goods are covered governs. § 9-303(c). Goods become covered by a certificate of title when a valid application for the certificate of title and the applicable application fee are delivered to the appropriate authority, and cease to be so covered when the certificate is no longer effective, or the goods become covered by a certificate of title issued by another jurisdiction. § 9-303(b).

The fifth exception is for deposit accounts. For security interests in deposit accounts, the local law of the bank's jurisdiction governs (determined as set forth in § 9-304(b), a definition which encourages designation of a jurisdiction in the agreement between a bank and its customer governing a deposit account).

A sixth exception contained in § 9-305 covers investment property. The debtor's location continues to govern for security interests in investment property perfected by filing and for certain automatically-perfected security interests in investment property. § 9-305(c). However, for security interests in investment property perfected by delivery or control, special rules are applicable. For a certificated security, the local law of the jurisdiction in which the security certificate is located governs. For an uncertificated security, the local law of the issuer's jurisdiction (within the meaning of § 8-110(d)) governs. For a security entitlement or securities account, the local law of the securities intermediary's jurisdiction (under § 8-110(e)) governs. For a commodity contract or commodity account, the local law of the commodity intermediary's jurisdiction (under § 9-305(b)) governs.

Finally, a seventh exception is included for letter-of-credit rights in § 9-306. Here the local law of the issuer's jurisdiction or the nominated person's jurisdiction (under § 5-116) governs.

A visualization of the general rule on choice of law and its exceptions follows:

CHOICE OF LAW							
GENERAL RULE § 9-301(1)	EXCEPTIONS						
	POSSESSORY SECURITY INTEREST	REAL-ESTATE RELATED COLLATERAL	TANGIBLE COLLATERAL	GOODS COVERED BY CERTIFICATE	DEPOSIT ACCOUNTS	INVESTMENT PROPERTY	LETTER-OF-CREDIT RIGHTS
LOCAL LAW OF JURISDICTION WHERE DEBTOR IS LOCATED GOVERNS PERFECTION, EFFECT OF PERFECTION OR NONPERFECTION AND PRIORITY OF SECURITY INTEREST § 9-307	LOCAL LAW OF JURISDICTION WHERE COLLATERAL IS LOCATED § 9-301(2)	FIXTURES, TIMBER TO BE CUT § 9-301(3)(A) & (B): LOCAL LAW OF JURISDICTION WHERE COLLATERAL IS LOCATED AS-EXTRACTED COLLATERAL § 9-301(4): LOCAL LAW OF JURISDICTION WHERE WELLHEAD OR MINEHEAD IS LOCATED	EFFECT OF PERFECTION OR NONPERFECTION AND PRIORITY GOVERNED BY LOCAL LAW OF JURISDICTION WHERE COLLATERAL IS LOCATED § 9-301(3)(C)	LOCAL LAW OF JURISDICTION UNDER WHOSE CERTIFICATE OF TITLE GOODS ARE COVERED § 9-303	LOCAL LAW OF BANK'S JURISDICTION § 9-304	CERTIFICATED SECURITY: LOCAL LAW OF JURISDICTION WHERE COLLATERAL IS LOCATED UNCERTIFICATED SECURITY: LOCAL LAW OF ISSUER'S JURISDICTION § 8-110(d) SECURITY ENTITLEMENT OR SECURITIES ACCOUNT: LOCAL LAW OF SECURITIES INTERMEDIARY'S JURISDICTION § 8-110(e) COMMODITY CONTRACT OR COMMODITY ACCOUNT: LOCAL LAW OF COMMODITY INTERMEDIARY'S JURISDICTION § 9-305(b) § 9-305	LOCAL LAW OF ISSUER'S JURISDICTION OR NOMINATED PERSON'S JURISDICTION § 5-116 § 9-306

Whenever you have rules that turn on the location of persons or things, you need guidance on what happens when the person or thing changes location. Section 9-316 provides that guidance for Article 9 choice of law purposes. There are four different situations addressed by § 9-316—a change in the location of the debtor, a change in the location of collateral subject to a possessory security interest, goods becoming covered a certificate of title that were perfected by another method under the law of another jurisdiction, and a change in the jurisdiction of a bank, issuer, nominated person, securities intermediary or commodity intermediary.

The first situation is when the location of the debtor governs perfection and the location of the debtor changes. There are two ways this can happen. One is if the debtor's location moves, for example because an individual changes his or her residence, or a registered organization changes its state of incorporation, or another organization changes its place of business (if it has only one) or chief executive office (if it has more than one). The second way the location of the debtor may change is by a transfer of the collateral to a person who thereupon becomes a "debtor," § 9-102(a)(28), by virtue of its interest in the collateral. This person may or may not be a "new debtor," § 9-102(a)(56) who becomes bound by the original security agreement under § 9-203(d).

The rules governing a change in location of the debtor are in § 9-316(a) and (b). A security interest properly perfected under the law of the debtor's original location remains perfected until the earliest of the time it would have been perfected under that law, and the end of the applicable grace period, which is four months for a change in the debtor's location and one year for a transfer of the collateral to a new person who becomes a debtor. After that period, unless the secured party perfects under the law of the newly-applicable jurisdiction, there are two consequences. The security interest becomes unperfected from that moment on, and the security interest is deemed never to have been perfected as against a "purchaser," § 1-201(b)(30), of the collateral for value (which would include a competing secured creditor whose security interest was perfected after the first secured creditor's security interest).

A visualization of the rules on change in the debtor's location follows:

CHANGE IN DEBTOR'S LOCATION § 9-316(a) - (b)			
EVENTS CAUSING CHANGE IN LOCATION		HOW LONG PERFECTION CONTINUES	RESULT OF FAILURE TO PERFECT UNDER NEW LAW WITHIN SPECIFIED PERIOD
DEBTOR CHANGES LOCATION TO NEW JURISDICTION	COLLATERAL MOVES TO NEW PERSON IN DIFFERENT JURISDICTION	EARLIEST OF TIME PERFECTION WOULD HAVE CEASED UNDER LAW OF ORIGINAL JURISDICTION AND: 1) FOR DEBTOR'S CHANGE IN LOCATION, FOUR MONTHS AFTER CHANGE 2) FOR TRANSFER OF COLLATERAL TO NEW PERSON WHO BECOMES DEBTOR, ONE YEAR AFTER TRANSFER	1) SECURITY INTEREST BECOMES UNPERFECTED AT END OF PERIOD, AND 2) SECURITY INTEREST IS DEEMED NEVER TO HAVE BEEN PERFECTED AS AGAINST A PURCHASER § 1-201(b)(30) FOR VALUE

The second situation in which the law governing perfection may change is when collateral in which a security interest is perfected by possession moves from one jurisdiction to another. In this case, § 9-316(c) provides no grace period for a secured party to perfect in the new jurisdiction. The security interest must be perfected (either by possession or otherwise) upon entry into the new jurisdiction.

A visualization of the rule on change in location of collateral subject to a possessory security interest follows:

CHANGE IN LOCATION OF COLLATERAL SUBJECT TO POSSESSORY SECURITY INTEREST § 9-316(c)		
EVENT CAUSING CHANGE IN LOCATION	HOW LONG PERFECTION CONTINUES	RESULT OF FAILURE TO PERFECT UNDER NEW LAW UPON ENTRY
COLLATERAL SUBJECT TO PERFECTED POSSESSORY SECURITY INTEREST IN ONE JURISDICTION IS BROUGHT INTO ANOTHER JURISDICTION	UNTIL TIME OF ENTRY INTO NEW JURISDICTION	SECURITY INTEREST BECOMES UNPERFECTED

The third situation in which the governing law for perfection of a security interest may change is when a security interest in goods is perfected under the law of one jurisdiction and those goods become covered by a certificate of title in another jurisdiction.

Section 9-316(d) states that the security interest remains perfected until it would have become unperfected under the law of the original jurisdiction. However, pursuant to § 9-316(e), if the secured party does not perfect its interest under the law of the new jurisdiction (by noting its interest on the certificate of title) before the earliest of the time the security interest would have become unperfected under the law of the original jurisdiction and four months after the goods become covered by the certificate of title, the security interest will become unperfected as against a "purchaser," § 1-201(b)(30), for value, and is deemed never to have been perfected as against a purchaser for value.

In addition, under § 9-337, if a certificate of title is issued by the new jurisdiction that does not show that the goods are subject to the security interest or state that they may be subject to security interests not shown thereon, two competing parties will prevail over the secured creditor even before the four-month period expires. The first is a buyer of the goods (other than one in the business of selling goods of that kind) who gives value and receives delivery without knowledge of the security interest. The other is a conflicting secured creditor who perfects a security interest in the goods without knowledge of the security interest.

A visualization of the rules on change in location of goods covered by a certificate of title follows:

CHANGE IN LOCATION OF GOODS COVERED BY A CERTIFICATE OF TITLE
§ 9-316(d) - (e)

EVENT CAUSING CHANGE IN LOCATION	HOW LONG SECURITY INTEREST REMAINS PERFECTED			RESULT OF FAILURE TO PERFECT UNDER NEW LAW WITHIN APPLICABLE PERIOD	
	AS AGAINST PURCHASER FOR VALUE	AS AGAINST NONPURCHASER	EXCEPTION § 9-337	AS AGAINST PURCHASER FOR VALUE	AS AGAINST NONPURCHASER
GOODS IN WHICH SECURITY INTEREST IS PERFECTED UNDER LAW OF ORIGINAL JURISDICTION BECOME COVERED BY CERTIFICATE OF TITLE IN NEW JURISDICTION	EARLIEST OF: 1) TIME SECURITY INTEREST WOULD BECOME UNPERFECTED UNDER LAW OF ORIGINAL JURISDICTION 2) FOUR MONTHS AFTER GOODS BECOME COVERED	TIME SECURITY INTEREST WOULD BECOME UNPERFECTED UNDER LAW OF ORIGINAL JURISDICTION	IF CERTIFICATE OF TITLE IS ISSUED THAT SHOWS NO SECURITY INTEREST, SECURED PARTY LOSES TO: 1) BUYER OF GOODS NOT IN BUSINESS OF SELLING GOODS OF THAT KIND WHO GIVES VALUE AND TAKES DELIVERY WITHOUT KNOWLEDGE 2) SECURED CREDITOR WHO PERFECTS SECURITY INTEREST WITHOUT KNOWLEDGE	1) SECURITY INTEREST BECOMES UNPERFECTED 2) SECURITY INTEREST IS DEEMED NEVER TO HAVE BEEN PERFECTED	NOT APPLICABLE

The final situation in which a change in the governing law may affect perfection is when the governing law is determined by the jurisdiction of some designated party other than the debtor—the bank, the issuer, a nominated person, a securities intermediary, or a commodity intermediary. The rules set forth in § 9-316(f) and (g) are the same as those provided for a change in the location of the debtor. A visualization of the rules relating to a change in the jurisdiction of a relevant person other than the debtor follows:

CHANGE IN RELEVANT PARTY'S LOCATION § 9-316(f) - (g)		
EVENT CAUSING CHANGE IN LOCATION	HOW LONG PERFECTION CONTINUES	RESULT OF FAILURE TO PERFECT UNDER NEW LAW WITHIN SPECIFIED PERIOD
BANK, ISSUER, NOMINATED PERSON, SECURITIES INTERMEDIARY OR COMMODITY INTERMEDIARY CHANGES JURISDICTION	EARLIEST OF TIME PERFECTION WOULD HAVE CEASED UNDER LAW OF ORIGINAL JURISDICTION AND FOUR MONTHS AFTER CHANGE	1) SECURITY INTEREST BECOMES UNPERFECTED AT END OF PERIOD, AND 2) SECURITY INTEREST IS DEEMED NEVER TO HAVE BEEN PERFECTED AS AGAINST A PURCHASER § 1-201(b)(30) FOR VALUE

Chapter 6
PRIORITY

The goal of a secured creditor is not only to obtain special rights as against the debtor in the event of a default (discussed in Chapter 11) but also to gain priority over potential competing claimants to the collateral. Except as otherwise provided in Article 9, a security interest is effective not only as between the debtor and secured party, but is also effective "against purchasers of the collateral, and against creditors." § 9-201(a). This means that a secured creditor will prevail against an unsecured creditor with respect to the collateral.

The basic priority rules of Article 9 are organized, for the most part, on the basis of the identity of the competing claimant. We will discuss them in the same way. We will then look at the exceptions that are included for particular types of collateral.

A. BASIC RULES OF PRIORITY

1. Secured Creditors

When a security interest or agricultural lien competes with another security interest or agricultural lien, there are three basic priority rules in § 9-322(a). First, a perfected security interest or agricultural lien prevails over an unperfected one. Second, as between two perfected security interests or agricultural liens, the first to file or perfect prevails. Third, as between two unperfected security interests or agricultural liens, the first to attach or become effective prevails. (For agricultural liens, the statute creating such liens may provide for different priority rules, § 9-322(g).) A visualization of the basic rules of priority for security interests follows:

BASIC PRIORITY RULES FOR COMPETING SECURITY INTERESTS § 9-322(a)		
	PERFECTED SECURITY INTEREST	UNPERFECTED SECURITY INTEREST
PERFECTED SECURITY INTEREST	FIRST TO FILE OR PERFECT PREVAILS § 9-322(a)(1)	PERFECTED SECURITY INTEREST PREVAILS § 9-322(a)(2)
UNPERFECTED SECURITY INTEREST	PERFECTED SECURITY INTEREST PREVAILS § 9-322(a)(2)	FIRST TO ATTACH OR BECOME EFFECTIVE PREVAILS § 9-322(a)(3)

There are special rules for applying these general principles to proceeds which we will discuss in Chapter 8.

2. Lien Creditors

A "lien creditor" is defined in § 9-102(a)(52) to mean a judgment lien creditor (a creditor who gets a lien on property by attachment, levy or the like), an assignee for the benefit of creditors, a trustee in bankruptcy, or a receiver in equity. A lien creditor, like a secured creditor, has a legally-cognizable property interest in the debtor's property subject to its lien. If that property is collateral for a security interest, a priority dispute may arise.

The priority rules for such conflicts are set forth in § 9-317(a). A perfected secured creditor always prevails over a lien creditor. An unperfected secured creditor will prevails over a lien creditor only if the secured creditor has satisfied one of the requirements for attachment set forth in § 9-203(b)(3) (the debtor has authenticated a security agreement or the secured party has taken possession or delivery or control of the collateral pursuant to a security agreement) *AND* has filed a financing statement. In all other cases, a lien creditor prevails over an unperfected secured creditor.

A visualization of the rules follows:

BASIC PRIORITY RULES FOR LIEN CREDITORS § 9-317(a)	
	LIEN CREDITOR
PERFECTED SECURITY INTEREST	PERFECTED SECURITY INTEREST PREVAILS
UNPERFECTED SECURITY INTEREST	LIEN CREDITOR PREVAILS UNLESS: 1) FINANCING STATEMENT IS FILED, AND 2) ONE OF CONDITIONS IN § 9-203(b)(3) IS SATISFIED

3. Buyers

Several priority rules bear on disputes between a secured creditor on the one side, and a buyer of the collateral on the other. The first set of rules specify when a buyer takes free of a security interest even if that security interest is perfected.

Section 9-320(a) allows a "buyer in ordinary course of business," other than a person buying farm products from a person engaged in farming operations, to take free of a security interest created by that buyer's seller. Commercial lawyers often refer to buyers in ordinary course of business as "BIOCOBs." A visualization of the requirements for the buyer to prevail follows:

**BASIC PRIORITY RULE FOR
BUYERS IN ORDINARY COURSE OF BUSINESS
§ 9-320(a)**

BUYER TAKES FREE OF SECURITY INTEREST IF:

1) BUYER IS "BUYER IN ORDINARY COURSE OF BUSINESS," § 1-201(b)(9)

2) BUYER DOES NOT BUY "FARM PRODUCTS," § 9-102(a)(34), FROM PERSON ENGAGED IN "FARMING OPERATIONS," § 9-102(a)(35)

3) SECURITY INTEREST WAS CREATED BY BUYER'S SELLER

The definition of "buyer in ordinary course of business" in § 1-201(b)(9) is a lengthy one, but sets out five basic requirements for a person to fall within the term. A visualization of the definition of "buyer in ordinary course of business" follows:

**BUYER IN ORDINARY COURSE OF BUSINESS
§ 1-201(b)(9)**

A PERSON WHO

1) BUYS "GOODS," § 9-102(a)(44)

2) IN GOOD FAITH

3) WITHOUT KNOWLEDGE THAT THE SALE VIOLATES THE RIGHTS OF ANOTHER PERSON IN THE GOODS

4) IN THE ORDINARY COURSE OF BUSINESS

5) FROM SELLER (NOT PAWNBROKER) IN BUSINESS OF SELLING GOODS OF THAT KIND

A buyer in ordinary course of business who satisfies the requirements of § 9-320(a) takes free of a security interest even if the buyer knows of its existence. Of course, if the buyer not only knows of its existence, but also knows that the sale violates the rights of the secured party, the buyer will not satisfy the requirements of § 1-201(b)(9) to be a "buyer in ordinary course of business" and therefore cannot take advantage of § 9-320(a).

A buyer cannot use § 9-320(a) to defeat the interest of a secured party in possession of the goods within the meaning of § 9-313. § 9-320(e).

Section 9-320(a) specifically excludes buyers of farm products from person engaged in farming operations. Buyers of farm products may, nevertheless, be protected by the Food Security Act of 1985 ("FSA"), 7 U.S.C. § 1631. The FSA contains its own definition of "buyer in the ordinary course of business" in § 1631(c)(1). Such a buyer need satisfy only three requirements. A visualization of the definition follows:

**BUYER IN THE ORDINARY COURSE OF BUSINESS
FOOD SECURITY ACT OF 1985
§ 1631(c)(1)**

PERSON WHO

1) BUYS "FARM PRODUCTS," § 1631(c)(5)

2) IN THE ORDINARY COURSE OF BUSINESS

3) SELLER ENGAGED IN FARMING OPERATIONS WHO IS IN BUSINESS OF SELLING FARM PRODUCTS

The general priority rule for the Food Security Act of 1985 is contained in § 1631(d), and like § 9-320(a) states that a buyer in the ordinary course of business generally takes free of a security interest created by the buyer's seller, even if it is perfected and even if the buyer knows of its existence.

However, § 1631(e) sets forth three situations in which the buyer of farm products takes subject to the security interest. Two are applicable if the relevant state has established a "central filing system," § 1631(c)(2), in which financing statements or notices are filed and compiled by the Secretary of State into a master list which is regularly distributed to each buyer of farm products, commission merchant and selling agent who registers with the Secretary of State. In such states, the buyer will not prevail against a secured party if the buyer fails to register with the Secretary of State prior to the purchase and the secured party has filed an effective financing statement or notice covering the farm products. § 1631(e)(2). The buyer will also lose in such states if the buyer receives a notice from the Secretary of State of the secured party's interest in the farm products being sold, and does not get a waiver or release from the secured party. § 1631(e)(3).

The third exception is applicable whether or not the state has a central filing system. The secured party will prevail if the buyer receives a notice of the security interest within one year before the sale of the farm products with the required information in it and specifying any payment obligations imposed on the buyer as a condition for waiver or release of the security interest, and the buyer fails to satisfy those payment obligations. § 1631(e)(1). A visualization of the priority rules for buyers in the ordinary course of farm products under the Food Security Act of 1985 follows:

<table>
<tr><td colspan="3" align="center">BASIC PRIORITY RULE FOR BUYERS IN THE ORDINARY
COURSE OF FARM PRODUCTS
FOOD SECURITY ACT OF 1985
7 U.S.C.A. § 1631</td></tr>
<tr><td align="center">RULE
§ 1631(d)</td><td colspan="2" align="center">EXCEPTIONS
§ 1631(e)</td></tr>
<tr><td rowspan="2">BUYER IN THE ORDINARY COURSE OF BUSINESS OF FARM PRODUCT FROM SELLER ENGAGED IN FARMING OPERATIONS TAKES FREE OF SECURITY INTEREST CREATED BY SELLER</td><td align="center">IN ALL STATES</td><td align="center">IN STATES WITH CENTRAL FILING SYSTEM</td></tr>
<tr><td>BUYER RECEIVES NOTICE FROM SELLER OR SECURED PARTY WITHIN ONE YEAR PRIOR TO SALE CONTAINING PAYMENT OBLIGATIONS FOR WAIVER OR RELEASE OF SECURITY INTEREST AND DOES NOT COMPLY</td><td>1) BUYER FAILS TO REGISTER AND EFFECTIVE FINANCING STATEMENT IS FILED, OR

2) BUYER RECEIVES NOTICE OF SECURITY INTEREST AND DOES NOT SECURE WAIVER OR RELEASE</td></tr>
</table>

One other type of buyer, other than the buyer in ordinary course of business, may prevail over even a perfected security interest. Under § 9-320(b), a buyer of goods from someone in whose hands the goods were "consumer goods" takes free of a security interest in those goods if four requirements are met. A visualization of the requirements follows:

BASIC PRIORITY RULE FOR
BUYER OF CONSUMER GOODS
§ 9-320(b)

BUYER OF CONSUMER GOODS TAKES FREE OF SECURITY INTEREST IF BUYER BUYS:

1) WITHOUT KNOWLEDGE OF SECURITY INTEREST

2) FOR VALUE

3) PRIMARILY FOR PERSONAL, FAMILY OR HOUSEHOLD PURPOSES

4) BEFORE FILING OF FINANCING STATEMENT

Section 9-320(b) is sometimes called the "consumer-to-consumer" provision, because the goods are "consumer goods" in the hands of the seller, and become "consumer goods" in the hands of the purchaser. The security interest in the goods may be perfected even without the filing of the financing statement because purchase-money security interests in consumer goods are automatically perfected under § 9-309(1). *See* Chapter 4.

As was true for the exception for buyers in the ordinary course of business, buyers of consumer goods cannot defeat possessory security interests. § 9-320(e).

A buyer may take free of a security interest that is *not* perfected under the circumstances described in § 9-317(b) and (d). For tangible collateral—tangible chattel paper, tangible documents, goods, instruments, or a security certificate—the buyer will prevail if the buyer gives value and receives delivery of the collateral without knowledge of the security interest (or agricultural lien) and before it is perfected. For intangible collateral—accounts, electronic chattel paper, electronic documents, general intangibles, or investment property other than a certificated security—the buyer will prevail if the buyer gives value without knowledge of the security interest (or agricultural lien) and before it is perfected. There is no delivery requirement, because intangible collateral cannot be delivered.

A visualization of the basic rules for buyers of collateral as against unperfected security interests follows:

BASIC PRIORITY RULE FOR BUYER COMPETING WITH UNPERFECTED SECURITY INTEREST § 9-317(b) & (d)	
TANGIBLE COLLATERAL § 9-317(b)	**INTANGIBLE COLLATERAL** § 9-317(d)
BUYER TAKES FREE IF: 1) GIVES VALUE 2) RECEIVES DELIVERY 3) WITHOUT KNOWLEDGE OF SECURITY INTEREST OR AGRICULTURAL LIEN 4) BEFORE IT IS PERFECTED	BUYER TAKES FREE IF: 1) GIVES VALUE 2) WITHOUT KNOWLEDGE OF SECURITY INTEREST OR AGRICULTURAL LIEN 3) BEFORE IT IS PERFECTED

4. Lessees or Licensees

Just as the "buyer in ordinary course of business" or BIOCOB, § 1-201(b)(9), can buy collateral free of a security interest created by its seller even if it is perfected, so too a "lessee in ordinary course of business" or LIOCOB, § 2A-103(1)(u), is given the right to take its leasehold free of a security interest in the goods created by its lessor, even if the security interest is perfected. § 9-321(c). A "licensee in ordinary course of business," § 9-321(a), is also allowed to take its rights under a nonexclusive license free of a security interest in the general intangible created by its licensor, even if the security interest is perfected. § 9-321(b).

A visualization of these lease and license counterparts to the rules for buyers in ordinary course of business follows:

BASIC PRIORITY RULES FOR LESSEES AND LICENSEES IN ORDINARY COURSE OF BUSINESS § 9-321	
LESSEES § 9-321(c)	**LICENSEES** § 9-321(b)
LESSEE TAKES FREE OF SECURITY INTEREST IN GOODS IF: 1) LESSEE IS "LESSEE IN ORDINARY COURSE OF BUSINESS," § 2A-103(1)(u), AND 2) SECURITY INTEREST WAS CREATED BY LESSOR	LICENSEE UNDER NONEXCLUSIVE LICENSE TAKES FREE OF SECURITY INTEREST IN GENERAL INTANGIBLE IF: 1) LICENSEE IS "LICENSEE IN ORDINARY COURSE OF BUSINESS," § 9-321(a), AND 2) SECURITY INTEREST WAS CREATED BY LICENSOR

If the lessee or licensee is competing with a security interest that is not perfected, § 9-317(c) and (d) provides rules comparable to those given buyers. A visualization of these rules follows:

BASIC PRIORITY RULE FOR LESSEE OR LICENSEE COMPETING WITH UNPERFECTED SECURITY INTEREST § 9-317(c) & (d)	
LESSEE § 9-317(c)	**LICENSEE** § 9-317(d)
LESSEE TAKES FREE IF: 1) GIVES VALUE, 2) RECEIVES DELIVERY, 3) WITHOUT KNOWLEDGE OF SECURITY INTEREST OR AGRICULTURAL LIEN, AND 4) BEFORE IT IS PERFECTED	LICENSEE OF GENERAL INTANGIBLE TAKES FREE IF: 1) GIVES VALUE, 2) WITHOUT KNOWLEDGE OF SECURITY INTEREST OR AGRICULTURAL LIEN, AND 3) BEFORE IT IS PERFECTED

B. SPECIAL PRIORITY RULES

1. Purchase-Money Security Interests

We already examined the definition of "purchase-money security interest," § 9-103(b), in connection with our discussion of § 9-109(1) which provides for automatic perfection of a purchase-money security interest (PMSI) in consumer goods. *See* Chapter 4.

Purchase-money security interests are also given special priority rules that enable their holders to prevail over prior perfected security interests, lien creditors, lessees and licensees notwithstanding the basic priority rules we have just covered.

The requirements for obtaining this priority over a competing secured creditor depends on the nature of the collateral in which the PMSI exists. If the collateral is goods other than inventory or livestock, § 9-324(a) allows the secured creditor with a PMSI to obtain priority if the PMSI is perfected when the debtor receives possession of the collateral or within 20 days thereafter.

If the collateral is inventory, the secured party holding a PMSI must take more steps to obtain priority. § 9-324(b). The PMSI must be perfected when the debtor receives possession of the inventory. In addition, if the holder of the conflicting security interest has filed a financing statement, the secured creditor must also send an authenticated notification to that conflicting holder (which is received within five years before the debtor receives possession of the inventory) stating that the secured party has or expects to have a PMSI in inventory of the debtor and describing the inventory.

If the collateral is livestock, the rules for priority are similar to those for inventory, except that the authenticated notification must be received within six months before the debtor receives possession of the livestock. § 9-324(d).

A visualization of the priority rules relating to purchase-money security interests and competing security interests follows:

B. SPECIAL PRIORITY RULES

PRIORITY OF PMSI COMPETING WITH NON-PMSI § 9-324		
NON-INVENTORY NON-LIVESTOCK § 9-324(a)	INVENTORY § 9-324(b)	LIVESTOCK § 9-324(d)
PMSI PREVAILS IF PERFECTED WHEN DEBTOR RECEIVES POSSESSION OF COLLATERAL OR WITHIN 20 DAYS THEREAFTER	PMSI PREVAILS IF: 1) PERECTED WHEN DEBTOR RECEIVES POSSESSION OF COLLATERAL, 2) PMSI HOLDER SENDS AUTHENTICATED NOTIFICATION TO OTHER SECURED PARTY, 3) NOTIFICATION RECEIVED WITHIN FIVE YEARS BEFORE DEBTOR RECEIVES POSSESSION OF COLLATERAL, AND 4) NOTIFICATION STATES THAT PMSI HOLDER HAS OR EXPECTS TO ACQUIRE PMSI AND DESCRIBES INVENTORY	PMSI PREVAILS IF: 1) PERECTED WHEN DEBTOR RECEIVES POSSESSION OF LIVESTOCK, 2) PMSI HOLDER SENDS AUTHENTICATED NOTIFICATION TO OTHER SECURED PARTY, 3) NOTIFICATION RECEIVED WITHIN SIX MONTHS BEFORE DEBTOR RECEIVES POSSESSION OF LIVESTOCK, AND 4) NOTIFICATION STATES THAT PMSI HOLDER HAS OR EXPECTS TO ACQUIRE PMSI AND DESCRIBES LIVESTOCK

If a PMSI is competing for priority with another PMSI, § 9-324(g) provides priority to the PMSI securing an obligation incurred as all or part of the purchase price of the collateral over one securing an obligation incurred for value given to enable the debtor to acquire rights in or use of collateral (i.e., the seller of the collateral prevails over a financer). In a competition between two sellers or between two financers, each holding a PMSI in the same collateral, the basic priority rules apply and the first to file or perfect will prevail under § 9-322(a). A visualization of the rules of § 9-324(g) follows:

PRIORITY OF PMSI COMPETING WITH PMSI § 9-324(g)	
SELLER v. FINANCER	OTHER CONFLICTS
SELLER HAS PRIORITY	RESOLVED BY PRIORITY RULES OF § 9-322(a)

If a buyer, lessee or lien creditor claims rights to collateral in which a secured party has a purchase-money security interest, the holder of the PMSI will prevail under § 9-317(e) if the holder files a financing statement with respect to the PMSI before or within 20 days after the debtor receives delivery of the collateral. The rule of § 9-317(e) is subject to the protection given to buyers in ordinary course of business and lessees in ordinary course of business under § 9-320 and § 9-321. A visualization of the rule of § 9-317(e) follows:

PRIORITY OF PMSI COMPETING WITH BUYER, LESSEE OR LIEN CREDITOR § 9-317(e)		
BUYER (NOT BIOCOB)	LESSEE (NOT LIOCOB)	LIEN CREDITOR
PMSI PREVAILS IF FINANCING STATEMENT FILED WITHIN 20 DAYS AFTER THE DEBTOR RECEIVES DELIVERY OF COLLATERAL	PMSI PREVAILS IF FINANCING STATEMENT FILED WITHIN 20 DAYS AFTER THE DEBTOR RECEIVES DELIVERY OF COLLATERAL	PMSI PREVAILS IF FINANCING STATEMENT FILED WITHIN 20 DAYS AFTER THE DEBTOR RECEIVES DELIVERY OF COLLATERAL

2. Future Advances

One of the great innovations of Article 9 was the flexibility it afford a secured creditor seeking to secure not only one extension of credit to an obligor but a series of advances. Section 9-204(c) explicitly validates security agreements providing that the collateral secures future advances, whether or not given pursuant to commitment. Official Comment 5 to § 9-204 states that the intention of the section was to reject cases excluding future advances from the secured obligations unless they were of the same or a similar type or class as earlier advances.

However, § 9-323 sets forth special priority rules for a security interest securing future advances when in competition with another security interest, with a lien creditor, with a buyer of goods, or with a lessee of goods. For a competing security interest, priority is generally determined, even with respect to the future advance, according to the general priority rules of § 9-322(a). However, priority with respect to the future advance dates only from the date of the future advance if the security interest securing such future advance is perfected automatically (either pursuant to § 9-309 or pursuant to the temporary perfection provisions of § 9-312) and is not made "pursuant to commitment," § 9-102(a)(68), entered into when perfection was by another means. § 9-323(a).

If the security interest securing a future advance is competing with a lien creditor, the secured creditor will prevail if the future advance satisfies any of three conditions—it is made not later than 45 days after the lien arose, it was made without knowledge of the lien, or it was made "pursuant to commitment," § 9-102(a)(68), entered into without knowledge of the lien. § 9-323(b).

If the security interest securing a future advance is competing with a buyer of goods (other than a buyer in ordinary course of business), the secured party will prevail if the future advance is made before the earlier of 45 days after the purchase or the date the secured party acquires knowledge of the purchase or, alternatively, is made "pursuant to commitment," § 9-102(a)(68), entered into before the earlier of 45 days after the purchase or the date the secured party acquires knowledge of the purchase. § 9-323(d) and (e).

Finally, if the security interest securing a future advance is competing with a lessee (other than a lessee in ordinary course of business), the secured party will prevail under the same circumstances as it would against a competing buyer. § 9-323(f) and (g).

A visualization of the rules relating to future advances follows:

PRIORITY RULES FOR SECURITY INTEREST SECURING FUTURE ADVANCES § 9-323			
COMPETING SECURITY INTEREST § 9-323(a)	COMPETING LIEN CREDITOR § 9-323(b)	COMPETING BUYER (NOT BIOCOB) § 9-323(d) & (e)	COMPETING LESSEE (NOT LIOCOB) § 9-323(f) & (g)
1) IF SECURITY INTEREST IS PERFECTED BY FILING, POSSESSION OR CONTROL: GENERAL RULES OF PRIORITY UNDER § 9-322(a) 2) IF SECURITY INTEREST IS PERFECTED AUTOMATICALLY: PRIORITY DATES FROM TIME ADVANCE IS MADE UNLESS MADE PURSUANT TO COMMITMENT ENTERED INTO WHILE PERFECTED BY ANOTHER MEANS	LIEN CREDITOR PREVAILS UNLESS: 1) ADVANCE MADE NOT LATER THAN 45 DAYS AFTER LIEN AROSE, OR 2) ADVANCE MADE WITHOUT KNOWLEDGE OF LIEN, OR 3) ADVANCE MADE PURSUANT TO COMMITMENT ENTERED INTO WITHOUT KNOWLEDGE OF LIEN	BUYER PREVAILS UNLESS: 1) ADVANCE MADE NOT LATER THAN 45 DAYS AFTER SALE WITHOUT KNOWLEDGE OF SALE, OR 2) ADVANCE MADE PURSUANT TO COMMITMENT ENTERED INTO NOT LATER THAN 45 DAYS AFTER SALE WITHOUT KNOWLEDGE OF SALE	LESSEE PREVAILS UNLESS: 1) ADVANCE MADE NOT LATER THAN 45 DAYS AFTER LEASE WITHOUT KNOWLEDGE OF LEASE, OR 2) ADVANCE MADE PURSUANT TO COMMITMENT ENTERED INTO NOT LATER THAN 45 DAYS AFTER LEASE WITHOUT KNOWLEDGE OF LEASE

3. Control Collateral

Article 9 contains some special priority rules that are applicable to certain types of collateral—deposit accounts, investment property, and letter-of-credit rights—as to which a secured party may perfect a security interest by control. In all cases, perfection by control prevails over perfection by another means.

The remaining rules resolve conflicts between competing secured creditors with control over the collateral. A visualization of these rules relating to collateral as to which one may perfect by control follows:

SPECIAL PRIORITY RULES FOR CONTROL COLLATERAL		
DEPOSIT ACCOUNTS § 9-327	INVESTMENT PROPERTY § 9-328	LETTER-OF-CREDIT RIGHTS § 9-329
1) SECURED PARTY WITH CONTROL PREVAILS OVER SECURED PARTY WITHOUT CONTROL	1) SECURED PARTY WITH CONTROL PREVAILS OVER SECURED PARTY WITHOUT CONTROL	1) SECURED PARTY WITH CONTROL PREVAILS OVER SECURED PARTY WITHOUT CONTROL
2) PRIORITY DETERMINED BY TIME OF OBTAINING CONTROL	2) PRIORITY DETERMINED BY TIME OF OBTAINING CONTROL OR SATISFYING CERTAIN REQUIREMENTS TO OBTAIN CONTROL	2) PRIORITY DETERMINED BY TIME OF OBTAINING CONTROL
3) BANK WITH WHICH DEPOSIT ACCOUNT IS MAINTAINED PREVAILS OVER COMPETING SECURITY INTEREST UNLESS CONTROL OBTAINED UNDER § 9-104(a)(3)	3) SECURITIES INTERMEDIARY WITH WHICH SECURITIES ACCOUNT IS MAINTAINED AND COMMODITY INTERMEDIARY WITH WHICH COMMODITY ACCOUNT IS MAINTAINED PREVAIL OVER COMPETING SECURITY INTEREST	
	4) AUTOMATICALLY PERFECTED SECURITY INTERESTS OF BROKERS, SECURITIES INTERMEDIARIES AND COMMODITY INTERMEDIARIES RANK EQUALLY	

4. Purchasers of Chattel Paper or Instruments

One can perfect a security interest in chattel paper or instruments either by filing or by taking possession of the collateral. Section 9-330 provides some special priority rules that enable certain secured creditors who take possession of the chattel paper or instruments to prevail over a prior security interest perfected by filing.

To obtain priority for a security interest in, or purchase of, chattel paper, a "purchaser," § 1-201(b)(30), must always give "new value," § 9-102(a)(57) and take possession of tangible chattel paper (or obtain control of electronic chattel paper) in good faith and in the ordinary course of the purchaser's business. The holder of a PMSI in inventory is deemed to give "new value" for chattel paper constituting proceeds of that inventory. § 9-330(e).

If the chattel paper is claimed merely as proceeds of inventory in which the competing secured party has a security interest, the purchaser who satisfies those two steps will prevail so long as the chattel paper does not indicate that it has been assigned to an identified assignee other than the purchaser (often called a "legend" on the chattel paper). § 9-330(a).

If the chattel paper is claimed *not* merely as proceeds but as primary collateral by the competing secured creditor, the purchaser who has satisfied those two requirements may prevail, but only if the purchaser does not have knowledge that the purchase violates the rights of the secured party. § 9-330(b). A legend on the chattel paper indicating that it has been assigned to an identified assignee other than the purchaser is deemed to provide the disqualifying knowledge. § 9-330(f).

A visualization of the special priority rules relating to chattel paper follows:

SPECIAL PRIORITY RULE FOR PURCHASERS OF CHATTEL PAPER § 9-330(a) & (b)	
PURCHASER, § 1-201(b)(30), OF CHATTEL PAPER PREVAILS OVER COMPETING SECURITY INTEREST IN CHATTEL PAPER IF: 1) PURCHASER GIVES NEW VALUE, § 9-102(a)(57), AND 2) TAKES POSSESSION OF TANGIBLE CHATTEL PAPER OR CONTROL OF ELECTRONIC CHATTEL PAPER IN GOOD FAITH AND IN THE ORDINARY COURSE OF THE PURCHASER'S BUSINESS	
IF CHATTEL PAPER CLAIMED MERELY AS PROCEEDS OF INVENTORY	IF CHATTEL PAPER NOT CLAIMED MERELY AS PROCEEDS OF INVENTORY
3) CHATTEL PAPER DOES NOT INDICATE THAT IT HAS BEEN ASSIGNED TO IDENTIFIED ASSIGNEE OTHER THAN PURCHASER	3) PURCHASER IS WITHOUT KNOWLEDGE (BY LEGEND ON CHATTEL PAPER OR OTHERWISE) THAT PURCHASE VIOLATES RIGHTS OF SECURED PARTY

The "purchaser," § 1-201(b)(30), of an instrument will prevail over a competing security interest in the instrument if the purchaser gives value and takes possession of the instrument in good faith and without knowledge that the purchase violates the rights of the secured party. § 9-330(d). As was true for chattel paper, the existence of a legend on the instrument indicating that it has been assigned to an identified secured party other than the purchaser, is deemed to give the purchaser knowledge that the purchase violates the rights of the secured party. § 9-330(f). A visualization of the special priority rule for purchasers of instruments follows:

**SPECIAL PRIORITY RULE FOR
PURCHASERS OF INSTRUMENTS
§ 9-330(d)**

PURCHASER, § 1-201(b)(30), OF INSTRUMENT PREVAILS OVER COMPETING SECURITY INTEREST IN INSTRUMENT IF:

1) PURCHASER GIVES VALUE,

2) TAKES POSSESSION OF INSTRUMENT IN GOOD FAITH AND IN THE ORDINARY COURSE OF THE PURCHASER'S BUSINESS, AND

3) PURCHASER IS WITHOUT KNOWLEDGE (BY LEGEND ON INSTRUMENT OR OTHERWISE) THAT PURCHASE VIOLATES RIGHTS OF SECURED PARTY

---

5. Transfers of Money

Money can serve as collateral for a secured obligation either as the principal collateral or as proceeds of other types of collateral. But money also constitutes a medium of exchange, § 1-201(b)(24), and security interests must not impede the free flow of funds in society. Therefore, under § 9-332, a transferee of money or of funds from a deposit account takes the money or funds free of a security interest unless the transferee acted in collusion with the debtor in violating the rights of the secured party. A visualization of the special priority rule for transfers of money follows:

SPECIAL PRIORITY RULE FOR TRANSFERS OF MONEY OR FUNDS FROM DEPOSIT ACCOUNTS § 9-332	
RULE	EXCEPTION
TRANSFEREE TAKES FREE OF SECURITY INTEREST	TRANSFEREE ACTS IN COLLUSION WITH DEBTOR IN VIOLATING RIGHTS OF SECURED PARTY

6. Possessory Liens

As a general matter, Article 9 applies only to transactions creating security interests by contract. § 9-109(a)(1). Therefore, § 9-109(d)(2) expressly excludes from the scope of Article 9 liens (other than agricultural liens) given by statute or other rule of law for services or materials. Nevertheless, Article 9 does have a special priority rule to resolve conflicts between certain of these non-contractual liens and those security interests within the scope of Article 9.

Section 9-333 defines "possessory liens" to which it relates, provides a rule of priority, and an exception to that rule. A visualization of the provisions dealing with possessory liens follows:

SPECIAL PRIORITY RULE FOR POSSESSORY LIENS § 9-333		
DEFINITION OF "POSSESSORY LIEN"	RULE	EXCEPTION
1) SECURES PAYMENT OR PERFORMANCE OF OBLIGATION FOR SERVICES OF MATERIALS FURNISHED WITH RESPECT TO GOODS IN ORDINARY COURSE OF BUSINESS, 2) CREATED BY STATUTE OR RULE OF LAW, AND 3) EFFECTIVENESS DEPENDS ON POSSESSION OF GOODS	POSSESSORY LIEN HAS PRIORITY OVER SECURITY INTEREST IN GOODS	1) LIEN IS CREATED BY STATUTE, AND 2) STATUTE EXPRESSLY PROVIDES THAT LIEN IS SUBORDINATE

7. Fixtures

The general scope provision of § 9-109(a)(1) states that Article 9 applies to transactions creating security interests in personal property or fixtures. Property rights arising in real property are covered by state real property law rather than Article 9. "Fixtures" are defined as goods that "have become so related to particular real property that an interest in them arises under real property law." § 9-102(a)(41). If those goods are subject to a security interest, the potential arises for conflicts between the Article 9 security interest and the interest in real property created under non-Article 9 law. Section 9-334 provides special priority rules to resolve that conflict.

The basic rule of § 9-334 is that the security interest in fixtures is subordinate to a conflicting "encumbrance," § 9-102(a)(32), including a mortgage and other lien on real property, or interest of an owner (other than the debtor) in the real property to which the fixtures are affixed. § 9-334(c). There are six exceptions to this basic rule, and one exception to an exception. Although each will be discussed in turn, a visualization of the structure of the priority rules follows:

SPECIAL PRIORITY RULE FOR SECURITY INTEREST IN FIXTURES COMPETING WITH REAL PROPERTY INTEREST (RPI) § 9-334		
RULE § 9-334(c)	**EXCEPTIONS**	**EXCEPTION TO EXCEPTION**
RPI PREVAILS OVER SECURITY INTEREST IN FIXTURES	FIRST IN TIME § 9-334(e)(1) PMSI § 9-334(d) READILY REMOVABLE GOODS § 9-334(e)(2) LIEN CREDITOR § 9-334(e)(3) MANUFACTURED HOME § 9-334(e)(4) CONSENT, DISCLAIMER, RIGHT TO REMOVE § 9-334(f)	CONSTRUCTION MORTGAGE § 9-334(h)

The first exception to the general priority rule is what I have called the "first in time" exception of § 9-334(e)(1). In order to take advantage of this exception, the secured creditor with a security interest in fixtures must satisfy three requirements. A visualization of the requirements for this exception follows:

FIRST IN TIME EXCEPTION
§ 9-334(e)(1)

---

1) SECURITY INTEREST IN FIXTURES IS PERFECTED

   • BY FIXTURE FILING, AND

   • BEFORE REAL PROPERTY INTEREST IS OF RECORD,

2) SECURITY INTEREST HAS PRIORITY OVER PREDECESSOR IN TITLE OF REAL PROPERTY INTEREST, AND

3) DEBTOR

   • HAS INTEREST OF RECORD IN REAL PROPERTY, OR

   • IS IN POSSESSION OF REAL PROPERTY

One of the requirements for this exception is the perfection of the security interest by a "fixture filing," defined in § 9-102(a)(40) as the filing of a financing statement covering goods that are or are to become fixtures and that satisfies the requirements of § 9-502(a) and (b). Financing statements filed as fixture filings must indicate that they cover fixtures, state that they are to be filed in the real estate records, describe the real property to which the fixtures are related and name a record owner of the real property (if the debtor does not have an interest of record).

If a financing statement is filed as a "fixture filing," § 9-501(a)(1)(B) directs that it be filed in the office designated for the filing or recording of a mortgage on the related real property. If a financing statement covers fixtures but is not filed as a "fixture filing," § 9-501(a)(2) provides that it may be filed centrally with all other financing statements. Either type of filing perfects the security interest in the fixtures, but to take advantage of the priority exception in § 9-334(e)(1), the security interest must be perfected by a fixture filing and therefore must be filed in the real estate records.

A visualization of the filing requirements for fixture filings follows:

FILING PROVISIONS FOR FIXTURE FILINGS	
REQUIREMENTS FOR FIXTURE FILING § 9-502(a) & (b)	FILING OFFICE FOR FIXTURE FILING § 9-501(a)(1)(B)
1) NAME OF DEBTOR	OFFICE DESIGNATED FOR FILING OR RECORDING OF MORTGAGE ON RELATED REAL PROPERTY
2) NAME OF SECURED PARTY OR ITS REPRESENTATIVE	
3) INDICATE COLLATERAL COVERED	
4) INDICATE THAT IT COVERS FIXTURES	
5) INDICATE THAT IT IS TO BE FILED IN REAL PROPERTY RECORDS	
6) DESCRIPTION OF REAL PROPERTY TO WHICH COLLATERAL IS RELATED	
7) IF DEBTOR DOES NOT HAVE RECORD INTEREST IN REAL PROPERTY, NAME OF A RECORD OWNER	

The second exception to the general rule of priority that subordinates security interests in fixtures to competing real property interests in the real property to which they are affixed is the exception for purchase-money security interests in fixtures in § 9-334(d). As is true of the other special priority rules in Article 9 dealing with purchase-money security interests, the special rule in § 9-334(d) allows a PMSI in goods that become fixtures to get priority over a prior conflicting interest, in this case a real property interest in the real property to which the goods are affixed. There are four requirements for the secured party to satisfy this exception.

Even if the secured party satisfies these requirements, however, there is an exception to the PMSI exception that allows a real property interest to prevail. The real property interest will prevail over a PMSI in fixtures if the real property interest is a construction mortgage and meets the requirements of § 9-334(h). The construction mortgage has no special priority over nonpurchase-money security interests that gain priority over real property interests by reason of another exception to the general rule. A visualization of the PMSI exception and the construction mortgage exception to the PMSI exception follows:

PMSI EXCEPTION AND CONSTRUCTION MORTGAGE EXCEPTION TO PMSI EXCEPTION		
PMSI EXCEPTION § 9-334(d)	CONSTRUCTION MORTGAGE § 9-334(h)	CONSTRUCTION MORTGAGE EXCEPTION § 9-334(h)
1) PMSI § 9-103, 2) REAL PROPERTY INTEREST AROSE BEFORE GOODS AFFIXED, 3) SECURITY INTEREST PERFECTED • BY FIXTURE FILING • NOT LATER THAN 20 DAYS AFTER GOODS AFFIXED, AND 4) DEBTOR HAS • INTEREST OF RECORD IN REAL PROPERTY, OR • IS IN POSSESSION OF REAL PROPERTY	1) SECURES OBLIGATION INCURRED FOR CONSTRUCTION OF IMPROVEMENT ON LAND, AND 2) RECORDED MORTGAGE INDICATES THAT IT IS CONSTRUCTION MORTGAGE	SECURITY INTEREST IN FIXTURES IS SUBORDINATE TO CONSTRUCTION MORTGAGE IF: 1) MORTGAGE IS RECORDED BEFORE GOODS AFFIXED, AND 2) GOODS BECOME FIXTURES BEFORE COMPLETION OF CONSTRUCTION

The third exception to the general rule favoring real property interests over security interests in fixtures is for fixtures that are readily removable and fall within one of three different categories of collateral. § 9-334(e)(2). If a secured party mistakenly believes that these readily removable goods are not fixtures and therefore files a regular financing statement before the goods become affixed, the exception allows the security interest to prevail over the competing real property interest even though the goods are subsequently determined to be fixtures. Of course, if the secured party had realized that the goods were to be fixtures, the secured party could have obtained priority over a subsequently-recorded real property interest by making a fixture filing, and could have obtained priority over a previously-recorded real property interest (not a construction mortgage) if the security interest was a PMSI and the secured party made a fixture filing within 20 days after the goods were affixed. A visualization of the readily removable goods exception follows:

READILY REMOVABLE GOODS EXCEPTION
§ 9-334(e)(2)

1) FIXTURES ARE READILY REMOVABLE,

2) FIXTURES ARE:

- FACTORY OR OFFICE MACHINES, OR

- EQUIPMENT NOT PRIMARILY USED OR LEASED FOR USE IN OPERATION OF REAL PROPERTY, OR

- REPLACEMENT OF DOMESTIC APPLIANCES THAT ARE CONSUMER GOODS, AND

3) SECURITY INTEREST IS PERFECTED (BY ANY MEANS) BEFORE GOODS AFFIXED

If the competing real property interest is a lien on the real property obtained by legal or equitable proceedings (a judicial lien), the security interest in fixtures will prevail as long as it was perfected by any means before the competing lien arose. § 9-334(e)(3). This would protect a security interest in fixtures perfected by a non-fixture filing against the trustee in bankruptcy for the debtor, among others. A visualization of the lien creditor exception follows:

LIEN CREDITOR EXCEPTION
§ 9-334(e)(3)

---

1) SECURITY INTEREST IS PERFECTED (BY ANY MEANS), AND

2) LEGAL OR EQUITABLE LIEN ARISES AFTER PERFECTION

The fifth exception is limited to security interests in "manufactured homes," § 9-102(a)(53), created in a "manufactured-home transaction," § 9-102(a)(54) (either one that creates a PMSI in a manufactured home or in which the manufactured home is the primary collateral). If such a security interest is perfected under a state certificate of title statute covering manufactured homes, it prevails over a competing real property interest in the real property to which the manufactured home becomes affixed. § 9-334(e)(4). A visualization of the exception follows:

MANUFACTURED HOME EXCEPTION
§ 9-334(e)(4)

---

1) SECURITY INTEREST IN MANUFACTURED HOME § 9-102(a)(53),

2) CREATED IN MANUFACTURED-HOME TRANSACTION § 9-102(a)(54), AND

3) SECURITY INTEREST PERFECTED UNDER APPLICABLE CERTIFICATE OF TITLE STATUTE

The final exception recognizes two situations in which the holder of the real property interest has consented, expressly or implicitly, to the priority of the security interest in fixtures attached to the real property. § 9-334(f). The first situation is when the holder of the real property interest authenticates a record consenting to the security interest or disclaiming an interest in the fixtures. The second situation is when the debtor has a right, as against the holder of the real property interest, to remove the fixtures from the real property. A visualization of the consent, disclaimer and right to remove exception follows:

CONSENT, DISCLAIMER, RIGHT TO REMOVE EXCEPTION
§ 9-334(f)

1) HOLDER OF REAL PROPERTY INTEREST CONSENTS TO SECURITY INTEREST OR DISCLAIMS INTEREST IN FIXTURES, OR

2) DEBTOR HAS RIGHT TO REMOVE GOODS AS AGAINST HOLDER OF REAL PROPERTY INTEREST

Although remedies will be discussed in Chapter 11, Article 9 contains a special provision dealing with remedies for a secured party secured by goods that are or are to become fixtures. Section 9-604(b) specifically allows a secured party to take advantage of remedies provided under real property law rather than Article 9 if the secured party chooses to do so. However, under § 9-604(c), a secured party with a security interest in fixtures that has priority over a competing real property interest always has the right to remove the collateral from the real property after a default. The secured party must reimburse the holder of the real property interest (other than the debtor) for any physical injury caused by the removal, but not for any diminution in value of the real property caused by the absence of the fixtures. A visualization of the remedies provided to the holder of a security interest in fixtures follows:

REMEDIES FOR HOLDER OF SECURITY INTEREST IN FIXTURES § 9-604	
REAL PROPERTY REMEDIES § 9-604(b)	ARTICLE 9 REMEDIES § 9-604(c) & (d)
SECURED PARTY MAY EXERCISE RIGHTS PROVIDED BY REAL PROPERTY LAW	SECURED PARTY WITH PRIORITY OVER REAL PROPERTY INTEREST MAY REMOVE FIXTURES UPON DEFAULT, PROVIDED THAT 1) SECURED PARTY MUST REIMBURSE HOLDER OF REAL PROPERTY INTEREST (OTHER THAN DEBTOR) FOR REPAIR OF PHYSICAL INJURY CAUSED BY REMOVAL, AND 2) HOLDER OF REAL PROPERTY INTEREST MAY DENY ACCESS UNLESS SECURED PARTY GIVES ADEQUATE ASSURANCE FOR PERFORMANCE OF OBLIGATION TO REIMBURSE

8. Accessions

Conceptually, accessions are very similar to fixtures. Whereas "fixtures," § 9-102(a)(41), are composed of goods that are affixed to real property, "accessions," § 9-102(a)(1) are composed of goods that are affixed to other goods in such a manner that their identity is not lost. A typical example would be an engine installed in a vehicle or aircraft. Section 9-335 deals with creation, perfection and priority of security interests in accessions, as well as remedies after default. A visualization of the rules relating to accessions follows:

SPECIAL PRIORITY RULES ON ACCESSIONS § 9-335					
CREATION	PERFECTION	PRIORITY			REMEDIES
			RULE	EXCEPTION	
SECURITY INTEREST IN ACCESSION MAY BE CREATED AND CONTINUES AFTER COLLATERAL BECOMES ACCESSION	IF SECURITY INTEREST IS PERFECTED WHEN COLLATERAL BECOME ACCESSION, IT REMAINS PERFECTED	PRIORITY IS DETERMINED AS FOR OTHER ART. 9 SECURITY INTERESTS	SECURITY INTEREST IN ACCESSION IS SUBORDINATE TO SECURITY INTEREST IN WHOLE PERFECTED UNDER CERTIFICATE OF TITLE STATUTE	ACCESSION SECURED PARTY WITH PRIORITY OVER INTERESTS IN WHOLE MAY REMOVE ACCESSION UPON DEFAULT, PROVIDED THAT 1) ACCESSION SECURED PARTY MUST REIMBURSE COMPETING PARTY (OTHER THAN DEBTOR) FOR REPAIR OF PHYSICAL INJURY CAUSED BY REMOVAL, AND 2) COMPETING PARTY MAY REFUSE PERMISSION TO REMOVE UNTIL SECURED PARTY GIVES ADEQUATE ASSURANCE FOR PERFORMANCE OF OBLIGATION TO REIMBURSE

9. Commingled Goods

"Commingled goods" are also goods that are physically united to other goods, but unlike "accessions," § 9-102(a)(1), commingled goods lose their identity in that union. § 9-336(a). As a result, a security interest in goods that become commingled goods cannot continue in the now-unidentifiable goods themselves. However, the security interest in the goods automatically attaches to the product or mass resulting from the commingling.

Section 9-336 deals with the creation and attachment, perfection and priority of security interests in commingled goods. A visualization of these rules follows:

COMMINGLED GOODS § 9-336			
CREATION AND ATTACHMENT	PERFECTION	PRIORITY	
		RULE	EXCEPTION
NO SECURITY INTEREST IN COMMINGLED GOODS AS SUCH, BUT SECURITY INTEREST MAY ATTACH TO RESULTING PRODUCT OR MASS IF COLLATERAL BECOMES COMMINGLED GOODS, SECURITY INTEREST ATTACHES TO PRODUCT OR MASS	IF SECURITY INTEREST IS PERFECTED WHEN COLLATERAL BECOMES COMMINGLED GOODS, SECURITY INTEREST THAT ATTACHES TO PRODUCT OR MASS IS PERFECTED	PRIORITY DETERMINED AS FOR OTHER ARTICLE 9 SECURITY INTERESTS	IF THERE IS MORE THAN ONE SECURITY INTEREST IN SAME PRODUCT OR MASS, 1) SECURITY INTEREST PERFECTED AT TIME COLLATERAL BECAME COMMINGLED GOODS HAS PRIORITY OVER SECURITY INTEREST THAT WAS UNPERFECTED 2) IF MORE THAN ONE SECURITY INTEREST WAS PERFECTED AT TIME COLLATERAL BECAME COMMINGLED GOODS, THEY RANK EQUALLY IN PROPORTION TO VALUE OF COLLATERAL AT TIME IT BECAME COMMINGLED GOODS

10. Right of Set-Off or Recoupment

Article 9 does not apply to rights of set-off or recoupment. § 9-109(d)(10). However, an Article 9 security interest in a "deposit account," § 9-102(a)(29), may come into conflict with the right of set-off or recoupment of the bank with which the deposit account is maintained. Section 9-340 resolves this conflict in favor of the bank unless the secured party has taken control of the deposit account pursuant to § 9-104(a)(3) by becoming the bank's customer with respect to the deposit account. A visualization of the special priority rule with respect to rights of set-off and recoupment follows:

SPECIAL PRIORITY RULE FOR RIGHT OF SET-OFF OR RECOUPMENT § 9-340	
RULE	EXCEPTION
BANK WITH WHICH DEPOSIT ACCOUNT IS MAINTAINED MAY EXERCISE RIGHT OF SET-OFF OR RECOUPMENT	BANK MAY NOT EXERCISE RIGHT OF SET-OFF OR RECOUPMENT IF SECURED PARTY HAS CONTROL OVER DEPOSIT ACCOUNT UNDER § 9-104(a)(3)

11. Federal Tax Liens

The United States is a creditor of every taxpayer, and if the taxpayer fails to pay taxes, the Internal Revenue Code provides for the imposition of a lien on all property and rights to property of the taxpayer. The federal tax lien statutes, 26 U.S.C. §§ 6321–23, provide not only for the imposition of the lien, but also its validity and priority as against competing creditors of the taxpayer. Among those competing creditors may be secured creditors with Article 9 security interests.

Although as a rule the federal tax lien arises at the time an assessment is made and continues until the liability is satisfied or becomes unenforceable, § 6322, the tax lien statutes provide exceptions to the validity of the tax lien for certain competing claims. There are two categories of claimants described in the exceptions in § 6323: those against whom a federal tax lien not valid if a notice of tax lien had been filed before their interests arose, and those against whom a federal tax lien is not valid even if a notice of tax lien had been filed when their interests arose.

A visualization of the rule and its exceptions follows:

FEDERAL TAX LIEN PRIORITY		
EFFECTIVENESS OF LIEN	LIEN NOT EFFECTIVE IF CLAIM ARISES BEFORE NOTICE OF TAX LIEN FILED	LIEN NOT EFFECTIVE EVEN IF CLAIM ARISES AFTER NOTICE OF TAX LIEN FILED
U.S. HAS LIEN ON ALL PROPERTY AND RIGHTS TO PROPERTY BELONGING TO TAXPAYER FROM TIME OF ASSESSMENT UNTIL LIABILITY SATISFIED § 6321 § 6322	1) PURCHASER 2) HOLDER OF A SECURITY INTEREST 3) MECHANIC'S LIENOR 4) JUDGMENT LIEN CREDITOR § 6323(a)	1) CERTAIN PURCHASERS OF A SECURITY, MOTOR VEHICLE, TANGIBLE PERSONAL PROPERTY 2) HOLDER OF SECURITY INTEREST IN SECURITY WITHOUT NOTICE OR KNOWLEDGE OF TAX LIEN 3) CERTAIN REAL PROPERTY LIENS 4) CERTAIN ATTORNEYS' LIENS 5) CERTAIN INSURERS 6) BANK WHICH MAKES LOAN WITHOUT NOTICE OR KNOWLEDGE OF TAX LIEN SECURED BY ACCOUNT AT THAT BANK § 6323(b)

Unlike the definition of "purchaser" in § 1-201(b)(30) of the Uniform Commercial Code, the definition of "purchaser" in § 6323(h)(6) explicitly excludes a person who acquires a security interest in property. Therefore, a secured creditor falls within the categories of persons against whom a tax lien is not effective only insofar as the secured creditor qualifies as a holder of a "security interest" within the meaning of § 6323(h)(1). This definition differs from that of "security interest" in § 1-201(b)(35) of the Uniform Commercial Code. Although, like the UCC definition, it represents an interest in property securing an obligation, it limits the definition in three respects. First, the property must be in existence for a security interest to exist. This means that the security interest does not exist with respect to after-acquired collateral until the collateral is acquired. Second, the interest in the property must be protected under local law against a subsequent judgment lien. Under the basic rule of priority dealing with conflicts between secured creditors and lien creditors, § 9-317(a), this means that either the security interest is perfected, or the secured creditor has satisfied one of the requirements of § 9-203(b)(3) and has filed a financing statement when the lien arises. Third, the security interest exists only to the extent the holder has parted with money or money's worth. This means that the security interest does not exist with respect to future advances until the advances are made.

A visualization of the definition of "security interest" under § 6323(h)(1) follows:

DEFINITION OF "SECURITY INTEREST" 26 U.S.C. § 6323(h)(1)	
BASIC DEFINITION	LIMITATIONS
INTEREST IN PROPERTY ACQUIRED BY CONTRACT TO SECURE PAYMENT OR PERFORMANCE OF AN OBLIGATION	1) PROPERTY IS IN EXISTENCE, 2) INTEREST IS PROTECTED AGAINST SUBSEQUENT JUDGMENT LIEN, AND 3) HOLDER HAS PARTED WITH MONEY OR MONEY'S WORTH

As described above, holders of "security interests" have priority over federal tax liens "until notice thereof which meets the requirements of [§ 6323(f)] has been filed," § 6323(a). The notice of tax lien is filed with respect to personal property in the same central filing office as Article 9 financing statements are filed. § 6323(f)(1)(A)(ii). A secured creditor can therefore search the records prior to extending credit to avoid unexpected subordination.

The filing requirements of the tax lien statutes create significant risks for Article 9 secured creditors. First, the choice of law provisions of the Internal Revenue Code do not coincide with the simplified choice of law rules of Article 9. Instead, for personal property, the Internal Revenue Service is directed to file a notice of tax lien in the state in which the property is located, § 6323(f)(1)(A)(ii), and personal property is deemed to be located "at the residence of the taxpayer at the time the notice of lien is filed." § 6323(f)(2)(B). Unlike the provisions of § 9-307 governing registered organizations, § 6323(f)(2) specifies that the "residence" of a corporation or partnership is the place of the "principal executive office," not the state under whose laws the organization is organized. Therefore, a search for tax liens may have to be conducted in a different jurisdiction from a search for UCC filings.

In addition, because the Internal Revenue Code does not include provisions comparable to § 9-503 and § 9-506 that condition the effectiveness of a financing statement on the accuracy of the debtor's name indicated thereon, courts may find a notice of lien effective even if the name of the taxpayer under which it is indexed does not comply with the requirements of § 9-503 and could not be found by a search under the taxpayer's correct name using the filing office's standard search logic.

The Internal Revenue Code also lacks provisions requiring new filings in the event a debtor's "residence" changes, comparable to § 9-316. Therefore, a searcher must potentially investigate more jurisdictions than would be required for a UCC search.

However, the limitations imposed by the definition of "security interest" in the tax lien acts leave even a secured creditor who has made an appropriate search and discovered no tax lien filing potentially exposed. There are three situations in which a secured creditor may be at risk.

The first is the secured creditor who takes a security interest not only in collateral existing at the time of attachment, but collateral acquired thereafter, for example, an inventory financer. Before the financer makes its first advance, it checks the appropriate filing office or offices and finds no tax lien notice. Therefore, when it makes its advance and does its own filing, its "security interest" in the inventory then in existence will prevail over any tax lien under § 6323(a). Assume a notice of tax lien is now filed. Then the debtor sells the inventory that existed prior to the filing of the notice and acquires new inventory with the proceeds. Because a "security interest" exists only if the collateral is in existence, the "security interest" in that new inventory arises only when the inventory was acquired. This "security interest" arose after the notice was filed, and therefore is not protected by § 6323(a).

Congress recognized that this risk would be unacceptable to those financing against collateral, like inventory and accounts, that "revolves" (that is, the collateral is sold or collected and replaced by new collateral). Therefore, Congress included special protection for certain types of property that are the subject of such financing transactions. § 6323(c). In order to be protected, the security interest that arises after the notice of tax lien is filed must meet three requirements. First, it must be in "qualified property." Second, it must be created by one of three types of agreements entered into before the notice of tax lien was filed. Third, it must be protected under local law against a subsequent judgment lien. A visualization of the requirements for protection of a secured creditor for after-acquired collateral follows:

PROTECTION FOR AFTER-ACQUIRED COLLATERAL 26 U.S.C. § 6323(c)				
PRE-NOTICE AGREEMENT	QUALIFIED PROPERTY			PROTECTED AGAINST JUDGMENT LIEN
	COMMERCIAL TRANSACTIONS FINANCING AGREEMENT	REAL PROPERTY CONSTRUCTION OR IMPROVEMENT FINANCING AGREEMENT	OBLIGATORY DISBURSEMENT AGREEMENT	
1) COMMERCIAL TRANSACTIONS FINANCING AGREEMENT, 2) REAL PROPERTY CONSTRUCTION OR IMPROVEMENT FINANCING AGREEMENT, OR 3) OBLIGATORY DISBURSEMENT AGREEMENT	1) COMMERCIAL FINANCING SECURITY • PAPER (INSTRUMENTS, CHATTEL PAPER, INVESTMENT PROPERTY, DOCUMENTS), • ACCOUNTS RECEIVABLE, • MORTGAGES, OR • INVENTORY, AND 2) ACQUIRED WITHIN 45 DAYS AFTER NOTICE OF TAX LIEN FILED	1) REAL PROPERTY AS TO WHICH CONSTRUCTION OR IMPROVEMENT IS BEING FINANCED, 2) CONTRACT TO CONSTRUCT OR IMPROVE REAL PROPERTY BEING FINANCED, AND 3) FARM CROP OR LIVESTOCK OR OTHER ANIMALS THE RAISING OR HARVESTING OF WHICH IS BEING FINANCED	PROPERTY EXISTING AT TIME OF NOTICE OF TAX LIEN AND PROPERTY ACQUIRED THEREAFTER DIRECTLY TRACEABLE TO OBLIGATORY DISBURSEMENT	1) PERFECTED, OR 2) ONE OF CONDITIONS IN § 9-317(a)(3) MET AND FINANCING STATEMENT

A "commercial transactions financing agreement" is defined in § 6323(c)(2)(A) as one that satisfies three requirements. A visualization of the definition follows:

DEFINITION OF "COMMERCIAL TRANSACTIONS FINANCING AGREEMENT"
26 U.S.C. § 6323(c)(2)(A)

1) AGREEMENT ENTERED INTO IN THE COURSE OF TRADE OR BUSINESS

2) PURPOSE OF AGREEMENT

- TO MAKE LOANS SECURED BY COMMERCIAL FINANCING SECURITY ACQUIRED BY TAXPAYER IN ORDINARY COURSE OF TRADE OR BUSINESS, OR

- TO PURCHASE COMMERCIAL FINANCING SECURITY (OTHER THAN INVENTORY) ACQUIRED BY TAXPAYER IN ORDINARY COURSE OF TRADE OR BUSINESS

3) LOAN OR PURCHASE IS MADE BEFORE EARLIER OF:

- 46th DAY AFTER DATE OF TAX LIEN FILING, OR

- DATE LENDER OR PURCHASER HAS ACTUAL NOTICE OR KNOWLEDGE OF TAX LIEN FILING

Therefore, a secured party who is financing or purchasing commercial financing security and makes a loan or purchase within 45 days after the notice of tax lien is filed without notice or knowledge of the tax lien filing will have priority over the United States with respect to collateral acquired within 45 days after the notice of tax lien filing if the security interest is perfected.

The second situation in which a secured creditor risks subordination to a tax lien by reason of the definition of "security interest" in § 6323(h)(1) is when the secured creditor makes future advances. The definition of "security interest" states that an interest qualifies only to the extent that the holder has parted with money or money's worth. Therefore, if a holder gives value prior to the filing of a notice of tax lien, it will be deemed to have a "security interest" to the extent of that value and will be protected by § 6323(a), but any value advanced after the filing will be deemed to create a new "security interest" which arises too late to benefit from § 6323(a) priority.

If the subsequent advance is pursuant to an "obligatory disbursement agreement," § 6323(c)(4) provides protection for the security interest represented by such advance, without regard to when it is made, both with respect to collateral existing at the time of the first advance and collateral that is directly traceable to the obligatory future advance.

If the subsequent advance is not pursuant to an "obligatory disbursement agreement," § 6323(d) provides protection for the advance to a similar extent as § 9-323 of the Uniform Commercial Code protects future advances against competing buyers or lessees. There are four requirements for protection under § 6323(d). A visualization of these requirements follows:

PROTECTION FOR FUTURE ADVANCES § 6323(d)	SECURITY INTEREST SECURING FUTURE ADVANCES VALID AGAINST TAX LIEN DESPITE FILING OF NOTICE IF:	COLLATERAL IS IN EXISTENCE WHEN NOTICE OF TAX LIEN FILED		
		COLLATERAL IS COVERED BY WRITTEN AGREEMENT ENTERED INTO PRIOR TO TAX LIEN FILING		
		ADVANCE IS MADE BEFORE EARLIER OF:	1) 46 DAYS AFTER FILING OF NOTICE OF TAX LIEN, OR	
			2) DATE SECURED PARTY HAS ACTUAL NOTICE OR KNOWLEDGE OF FILING	
		SECURITY INTEREST IS PERFECTED		

The final situation in which a secured party seems to risk subordination to a tax lien upon filing of a notice by the United States is when the secured party holds a purchase-money security interest, having sold collateral to the taxpayer or financed the acquisition of collateral by the taxpayer after a notice of tax lien was filed. Although there is nothing in the Internal Revenue Code tax lien statutes addressing this concern, Rev. Rul. 68-57 indicates that the government considers the taxpayer to have acquired the new collateral subject to the secured party's PMSI, and therefore the PMSI has priority over the tax lien that attaches to the property upon its acquisition by the taxpayer.

Chapter 7
BANKRUPTCY

When a debtor files for protection under the Bankruptcy Code, 11 U.S.C. § 101, et seq., the secured creditor's position is determined not only by its compliance with the provisions of Article 9 but also by the rights and duties imposed by the Bankruptcy Code. There are three different chapters of the Bankruptcy Code under which most filings are made: chapter 7 (which provides for liquidations of assets of individuals and other entities), chapter 13 (which provides for debt repayment plans for individuals with regular income and limited debts) and chapter 11 (which provides for reorganizations). In this chapter we will focus on those aspects of the Bankruptcy Code that impact secured creditors and their collateral, both during the bankruptcy case and thereafter. Except as otherwise specified, all references to a "Section" in this chapter is to a section of the Bankruptcy Code.

A. IMPACT OF BANKRUPTCY PETITION

The filing of a bankruptcy petition creates "an estate" comprised of, among other property, "all legal or equitable interests of the debtor in property as of the commencement of the case" and "proceeds, product, offspring, rents, or profits of or from" estate property." Section 541. This property becomes part of the bankruptcy estate no matter where it is located and even if it is held by someone other than the debtor. In fact, Section 542 requires that someone in "possession, custody, or control" of estate property must turn it over to the trustee in bankruptcy. Thus, all collateral in which a debtor has any legal or beneficial interest falls within the definition of "estate" property, and a secured creditor in possession or control of collateral must delivery it to the trustee.

The bankruptcy filing also triggers the application of the so-called "automatic stay" described in Section 362. Section 362 specifies certain acts that are automatically stayed, and certain acts that may continue notwithstanding the stay. Almost all of the acts specifically barred might be applicable to a secured creditor. Only one of the exceptions is directed at secured creditors. It allows a secured creditor to perfect its security interest up to 30 days after attachment despite the intervention of the bankruptcy filing. A visualization of the relevant acts applicable to secured creditors follows:

IMPACT OF AUTOMATIC STAY ON SECURED CREDITOR § 362	
STAYED § 362(a)	**NOT STAYED** § 362(b)
1) COMMENCEMENT OR CONTINUATION OF PREPETITION ACTION OR PROCEEDING AGAINST DEBTOR OR TO RECOVER PREPETITION CLAIM 2) ENFORCEMENT AGAINST DEBTOR OR PROPERTY OF ESTATE OF PREPETITION JUDGMENT 3) ACT TO OBTAIN POSSESSION OF OR EXERCISE CONTROL OVER PROPERTY OF ESTATE 4) ACT TO CREATE, PERFECT OR ENFORCE LIEN AGAINST PROPERTY OF ESTATE 5) ACT TO CREATE, PERFECT OR ENFORCE LIEN SECURING PREPETITION CLAIM AGAINST PROPERTY OF DEBTOR 6) ACT TO COLLECT, ASSESS OR RECOVER PREPETITION CLAIM 7) SETOFF OF PREPETITION DEBT OWING TO DEBTOR AGAINST CLAIM AGAINST DEBTOR	PERFECTION OF INTEREST IN PROPERTY TO EXTENT TRUSTEE'S POWERS ARE SUBJECT TO THAT PERFECTION UNDER § 546(b) OR PERFECTION TAKES PLACE WITHIN 30 DAYS AFTER ATTACHMENT § 362(b)(3)

B. DETERMINATION OF SECURED STATUS

The extent to which a secured creditor will be treated as having a secured claim in a bankruptcy case is determined by Section 506(a). Section 506(a)(1) states that a creditor's allowed claim secured by a lien on property or subject to setoff is a "secured claim" only "to the extent of the value of such creditor's interest in the estate's interest in such property, or to the extent of the amount subject to setoff." If such value is less than the amount of the allowed claim, any amount by which the claim exceeds the value is treated as unsecured. For example, if the estate includes collateral with a value of $5 million securing a debt then outstanding in the amount of $5 million, all of the debt would be treated as a secured claim. If the $5 million of collateral secures a debt then outstanding in the amount of $6 million, only $5 million of that debt would be a secured claim. The remaining $1 million of the debt would be treated as an unsecured claim. The result of Section 506(a)(1) is to bifurcate an undersecured claim into two different claims, a secured claim to the extent of the value of the collateral, and an unsecured claim for the remainder of the claim.

B. DETERMINATION OF SECURED STATUS

Valuation of the collateral will always be a key focus of Section 506(a)(1). Congress has provided the valuation method for a bankruptcy case involving an individual debtor in chapter 7 or chapter 13, stating in Section 506(a)(2) that value should be determined "based on the replacement value of such property as of the date of the filing of the petition without deduction for costs of sale or marketing." If that property is acquired for personal, family or household purposes, replacement value is "the price a retail merchant would charge for property of that kind considering the age and condition of the property at the time value is determined." For situations not covered by Section 506(a)(2), Section 506(a)(1) states that value "shall be determined in light of the purpose of the valuation and of the proposed disposition or use of such property."

If a secured claim is oversecured (meaning the value of the collateral exceeds the amount of the allowed claim), Section 506(b) permits the holder of the claim to receive interest on the claim and any reasonable fees, costs or charges provided for under the agreement or state statute under which the claim arose.

A visualization of these provisions follows:

DETERMINATION OF SECURED STATUS § 506					
SECURED CLAIM § 506(a)(1)		VALUATION § 506(a)(1) & (2)		INTEREST § 506(b)	
UNDERSECURED	FULLY SECURED	INDIVIDUAL DEBTOR IN CH. 7 OR 13 CASE	OTHER CASES	UNDERSECURED	FULLY SECURED
CLAIM IS SECURED TO EXTENT OF VALUE OF CREDITOR'S INTEREST IN ESTATE'S INTEREST IN PROPERTY; REMAINING CLAIM IS UNSECURED	CLAIM IS SECURED CLAIM TO FULL EXTENT OF CLAIM	REPLACEMENT VALUE OF PERSONAL PROPERTY AS OF DATE OF FILING OF PETITION WITHOUT DEDUCTION FOR COSTS OF SALE OR MARKETING	VALUE DETERMINED IN LIGHT OF PURPOSE OF VALUATION AND OF PROPOSED DISPOSITION OR USE OF PROPERTY	NO INTEREST ALLOWED	HOLDER ALLOWED INTEREST ON CLAIM AND ANY REASONABLE FEES, COSTS, OR CHARGES PROVIDED UNDER THE AGREEMENT OR STATUTE GIVING RISE TO CLAIM

C. POST-PETITION EFFECT OF SECURITY INTEREST

Although a security interest that is not avoidable in bankruptcy will remain effective with respect to collateral existing at the time of the bankruptcy filing, Section 552 states that it will not attach to any property acquired after the commencement of the bankruptcy case. There is, however, an exception to this general rule. If the postpetition property constitutes proceeds, products, offspring, or profits of the collateral and becomes subject to a security interest created by a pre-bankruptcy security agreement, the postpetition property will also become collateral unless the court, based on the equities of the case, orders otherwise.

A visualization of the provisions of Section 552 as it relates to personal property security interests follows:

SECURITY INTEREST AFTER BANKRUPTCY § 552		
RULE § 552(a)	EXCEPTION § 552(b)(1)	EXCEPTIONS TO EXCEPTION
PRE-FILING SECURITY INTEREST DOES NOT ATTACH TO PROPERTY ACQUIRED POST-FILING	1) PROPERTY IS PROCEEDS, PRODUCTS, OFFSPRING OR PROFITS OF COLLATERAL, 2) PRE-FILING SECURITY AGREEMENT, AND 3) SECURITY INTEREST COVERS PROCEEDS, PRODUCTS, OFFSPRING OR PROFITS	1) AVOIDING POWERS OF TRUSTEE 2) COURT, BASED ON EQUITIES OF CASE, ORDERS OTHERWISE

We will look at proceeds in Chapter 8.

D. TREATMENT OF COLLATERAL DURING BANKRUPTCY CASE

What happens to the collateral while the bankruptcy case is pending? Because of the automatic stay, the secured party may not exercise any remedies with respect to the collateral unless the bankruptcy judge permits the secured party to do so. A secured party who wishes to exercise such remedies seeks "relief from the stay" under Section 362(d). In order to succeed in such a request, the secured party must establish one of four grounds for relief specified in that section. A visualization of the provisions of Section 362(d) follows:

GROUNDS FOR RELIEF FROM AUTOMATIC STAY			
§ 362(d)(1)	§ 362(d)(2)	§ 362(d)(3)	§ 362(d)(4)
FOR CAUSE, INCLUDING LACK OF ADEQUATE PROTECTION, § 361, OF AN INTEREST IN PROPERTY	WITH RESPECT TO PROPERTY: 1) DEBTOR DOES NOT HAVE EQUITY IN SUCH PROPERTY, AND 2) PROPERTY IS NOT NECESSARY TO AN EFFECTIVE REORGANIZATION	WITH RESPECT TO SINGLE ASSET REAL ESTATE, § 101(51B), DEBTOR HAS NOT WITHIN 90 DAYS (OR 30 DAYS AFTER COURT FINDS SECTION APPLICABLE TO DEBTOR) EITHER 1) FILED A PLAN OF REORGANIZATION WITH REASONABLE POSSIBILITY OF CONFIRMATION, OR 2) COMMENCED MONTHLY PAYMENTS AT NONDEFAULT CONTRACT RATE OF INTEREST	WITH RESPECT TO REAL PROPERTY, IF COURT FINDS PETITION WAS PART OF SCHEME TO HINDER, DELAY OR DEFRAUD CREDITORS THAT INVOLVED EITHER: 1) TRANSFER OF INTEREST IN REAL PROPERTY WITHOUT CONSENT OF SECURED CREDITOR, OR 2) MULTIPLE BANKRUPTCY FILINGS

If the secured creditor does not seek, or is unable to obtain, relief from the stay, the trustee in bankruptcy may be able to use, sell or lease the collateral subject to the requirements of Section 363. If the debtor's business continues to operate during bankruptcy, generally Section 363 allows the trustee to use property of the estate, and enter into transactions with respect to that property, in the ordinary course of business without notice or a hearing. Section 363(c)(1). If the use, sale or lease of property is not in the ordinary course, the trustee may take the action only after notice and a hearing. Section 363(b)(1).

D. TREATMENT OF COLLATERAL DURING BANKRUPTCY CASE

However, if an entity other than the debtor has an interest (such as a security interest) in the property the trustee proposes to use, sell or lease, that entity may request that the court prohibit the trustee's action, or condition its permission on the provision of adequate protection to the entity with the interest. Section 363(e). "Adequate protection" is described in Section 361, and may include a cash payment or payments, additional or replacement liens, or other relief resulting in the realization of the "indubitable equivalent" of the entity's interest in the property.

The trustee may not sell property in which another entity has an interest unless one of the five conditions of Section 363(f) are satisfied.

If the property the trustee seeks to use, sell or lease is "cash collateral" (defined in Section 363(a) to include cash, negotiable instruments, documents of title, securities, deposit accounts, or other cash equivalents), Section 363(c)(2) bars the trustee from taking such action unless either the entity with an interest in the cash collateral consents, or the court, after notice and a hearing, authorizes the action. The court will not authorize such action unless the interest of the secured party is adequately protected.

A visualization of the provisions relating to use, sale or lease of property follows:

USE, SALE OR LEASE OF PROPERTY § 363			
PROPERTY OF THE ESTATE		**PROPERTY SUBJECT TO INTEREST OF ANOTHER ENTITY**	**CASH COLLATERAL**
TRUSTEE MAY ENTER INTO TRANSACTIONS IN THE ORDINARY COURSE OF BUSINESS § 363(c)(1)	TRUSTEE MAY ENTER INTO TRANSACTIONS OUTSIDE ORDINARY COURSE OF BUSINESS WITH NOTICE AND HEARING § 363(b)(1)	USE, SALE OR LEASE MAY BE PROHIBITED OR CONDITIONED ON PROVISION OF ADEQUATE PROTECTION § 363(e) SALE PROHIBITED UNLESS: 1) PERMITTED BY APPLICABLE NON-BANKRUPTCY LAW 2) ENTITY CONSENTS 3) SOLD FOR PRICE GREATER THAN ALL LIENS 4) INTEREST IN BONA FIDE DISPUTE 5) ENTITY CAN BE COMPELLED TO ACCEPT MONEY § 363(f)	TRUSTEE MAY USE, SELL OR LEASE ONLY WITH CONSENT, OR WITH COURT APPROVAL § 363(c)(2)

E. AVOIDING POWERS

The Bankruptcy Code gives the debtor or the trustee in bankruptcy the authority to undo certain prepetition transactions. The provisions conferring this ability are often called the "avoiding powers." We will look at those provisions that may be used to attack the security interest of, or payments made to, a secured creditor.

1. Avoidance of Lien Impairing Exemption

The individual debtor (a living, breathing person) is authorized by Section 522(b) of the Bankruptcy Code to claim certain property as exempt from property of the estate, either by application of federal exemption law or under state exemption law. Although a debtor may voluntarily encumber personal property that would be exempt from execution, and these voluntarily-incurred security interests are generally enforceable in bankruptcy, there is one situation in which the debtor may avoid a valid security interest merely because it denies the debtor the full exemption to which he or she would otherwise be entitled.

Under Section 522(f)(1)(B), an individual debtor may avoid the fixing of a "nonpossessory, nonpurchase-money security interest" in three different types of potentially exempt property to the extent the lien impairs an exemption. To the extent the security interest is avoided, the secured creditor will be relegated to an unsecured claim against the debtor's (nonexempt) estate. The justification for this avoiding power is that the type of property involved has very little economic value to a secured creditor who did not finance its acquisition (the security interest is not a purchase-money security interest), but has tremendous emotional value to the debtor. This disparity creates "hostage value" to the creditor, and Congress did not want secured creditors to be able to take advantage of that position in bankruptcy.

A visualization of Section 522(f)(1)(B) follows.

AVOIDANCE OF SECURITY INTERESTS IMPAIRING EXEMPTION § 522(f)(1)(B)		
TYPE OF LIEN	TYPE OF PROPERTY	COMPUTATION OF IMPAIRMENT § 522(f)(2)
NONPOSSESSORY, NONPURCHASE-MONEY SECURITY INTEREST	1) HOUSEHOLD FURNISHINGS, HOUSEHOLD GOODS, WEARING APPAREL, APPLIANCES, BOOKS, ANIMALS, CROPS, MUSICAL INSTRUMENTS, JEWELRY HELD PRIMARILY FOR PERSONAL, FAMILY OR HOUSEHOLD USE BY DEBTOR OR DEPENDENT, 2) IMPLEMENTS, PROFESSIONAL BOOKS OR TOOLS OF THE TRADE OF DEBTOR OR DEPENDENT, OR 3) PROFESSIONALLY PRESCRIBED HEALTH AIDS FOR DEBTOR OR DEPENDENT	SUM OF: 1) CHALLENGED LIEN 2) ALL OTHER LIENS 3) AMOUNT OF EXEMPTION MINUS VALUE OF INTEREST OF DEBTOR IN PROPERTY WITHOUT ANY LIENS

Section 522(f)(4) includes a detailed definition of the term "household goods" as used in the avoidance provision.

2. Strong-Arm Clause

The so-called "strong-arm clause" is the power given to the trustee in bankruptcy under Section 544(a) to avoid "transfers," Section 101(54), of property of the debtor (which include the creation of security interests), or obligations incurred by the debtor, that could be avoided by three different classes of persons outside of bankruptcy. Those three categories include a creditor obtaining a judicial lien on all property of the debtor as of the commencement of the bankruptcy case. The importance of this power to a secured creditor lies in the basic rules of priority we have already discussed. Under UCC § 9-317(a)(2), a lien creditor will prevail over a security interest or agricultural lien if the judicial lien arises before the security interest or agricultural lien is perfected, or before the holder has both filed a financing statement and satisfied one of the requirements for attachment listed in UCC § 9-203(b)(3). Therefore, under Section 544(a), the trustee in bankruptcy is treated as a judicial lien creditor and can avoid a security interest or agricultural lien that is unperfected as of the time of bankruptcy.

There is one exception to the trustee's avoiding power under Section 544(a). Section 546(b)(1) makes the trustee's powers subject to "any generally applicable law that . . . permits perfection of an interest in property to be effective against an entity that acquires rights in such property before the date of perfection." Because UCC § 9-317(e) allows the holder of a purchase-money security interest to perfect its interest within 20 days after the debtor receives delivery of the collateral and makes that perfection effective against a judgment lien creditor whose lien arises before the date of perfection, the trustee may not avoid a PMSI that is unperfected at the time of the filing of the bankruptcy case but that is perfected thereafter within 20 days after the debtor receives delivery of the collateral.

A visualization of the strong-arm clause follows:

STRONG-ARM CLAUSE § 544(a)	
RIGHTS AND POWERS OF TRUSTEE	EXCEPTION § 546(b)(1)
MAY AVOID ANY TRANSFER OF PROPERTY OR OBLIGATION INCURRED BY DEBTOR VOIDABLE BY HYPOTHETICAL: 1) JUDICIAL LIEN CREDITOR AS OF COMMENCEMENT OF CASE, 2) UNSATISFIED EXECUTION CREDITOR AS OF COMMENCEMENT OF CASE, OR 3) BONA FIDE PERFECTED PURCHASER OF REAL PROPERTY AS OF COMMENCEMENT OF CASE	ANY GENERALLY APPLICABLE LAW THAT PERMITS PERFECTION OF INTEREST IN PROPERTY TO BE EFFECTIVE AGAINST ENTITY ACQUIRING RIGHTS BEFORE PERFECTION

3. Fraudulent Transfer or Obligation

The Bankruptcy Code provides the trustee in bankruptcy two different bases for avoiding fraudulent transfers or obligations. The first is Section 548, which allows the trustee to avoid "transfers," Section 101(54), of an interest of the debtor in property or obligations incurred by the debtor that satisfy two requirements. The first is that the transfer must have been made or obligation incurred on or within two years before the date of the filing of the petition commencing the bankruptcy case. The second is that the transfer or incurrence of the obligation can be labeled "fraud," either actual fraud or constructive fraud. Actual fraud involves an intent to "hinder, delay, or defraud" a present or future creditor of the debtor. Constructive fraud is not fraud at all in any moral sense, but is the result of a transaction in which the debtor received less than a reasonably equivalent value in exchange, and was financially troubled at the time or was engaging in conduct benefitting an insider. A visualization of the requirements for a fraudulent transfer or obligation under Section 548 follows:

FRAUDULENT TRANSFER OR OBLIGATION **§ 548**	
TRUSTEE MAY AVOID TRANSFER OF INTEREST IN DEBTOR'S PROPERTY OR OBLIGATION INCURRED BY DEBTOR IF: 1) MADE OR INCURRED ON OR WITHIN TWO YEARS BEFORE FILING OF PETITION, AND 2) ACTUAL OR CONSTRUCTIVE FRAUD	
ACTUAL FRAUD	CONSTRUCTIVE FRAUD
ACTUAL INTENT TO HINDER, DELAY, OR DEFRAUD ANY PRESENT OR FUTURE CREDITOR OF DEBTOR	1) DEBTOR RECEIVED LESS THAN A REASONABLY EQUIVALENT VALUE IN EXCHANGE, AND 2) EITHER: • DEBTOR WAS INSOLVENT OR WAS RENDERED INSOLVENT, • DEBTOR'S REMAINING PROPERTY WAS UNREASONABLY SMALL CAPITAL FOR BUSINESS OR TRANSACTION, • DEBTOR INTENDED TO INCUR OR BELIEVED WOULD INCUR DEBTS BEYOND ABILITY TO PAY, OR • TRANSACTION WAS TO OR FOR BENEFIT OF INSIDER UNDER EMPLOYMENT CONTRACT NOT IN ORDINARY COURSE OF BUSINESS

The second means by which a trustee in bankruptcy may avoid a fraudulent transfer or obligation is under Section 544(b), which allows the trustee to avoid any "transfer," Section 101(54), of an interest of the debtor in property or any obligation incurred by the debtor that could be avoided by a creditor holding an allowable unsecured claim under applicable non-bankruptcy law. Although unsecured creditors are generally unable under applicable non-bankruptcy law (UCC § 9-201(a)) to prevail over security interests, unsecured creditor may be able to attack security interests as a transfer of an interest in debtor's property under state fraudulent transfer laws. Therefore, if there is an actual unsecured creditor in the debtor's bankruptcy case who would be able to assert an avoidance action under the relevant state fraudulent transfer statute, the trustee may step into the shoes of that unsecured creditor (be subrogated to that creditor's rights) and bring the avoidance action on behalf of the estate.

The Uniform Fraudulent Transfer Act, which has been enacted by most states, allows unsecured creditors to avoid transfers made or obligations incurred if the transactions demonstrate either actual fraud or constructive fraud. Certain of these transactions may be challenged only by persons who were creditors whose claims arose before the transaction took place (present creditors). Others may be challenged by both present and future creditors.

A visualization of the requirements for avoidance of a transfer or obligation under the Uniform Fraudulent Transfer Act follows:

FRAUDULENT TRANSFER OR OBLIGATION UNIFORM FRAUDULENT TRANSFER ACT			
PRESENT AND FUTURE CREDITORS § 4		PRESENT CREDITORS § 5	
ACTUAL FRAUD	CONSTRUCTIVE FRAUD	CONSTRUCTIVE FRAUD	PREFERENCE
ACTUAL INTENT TO HINDER, DELAY, OR DEFRAUD ANY PRESENT OR FUTURE CREDITOR OF DEBTOR	1) DEBTOR DID NOT RECEIVE A REASONABLY EQUIVALENT VALUE IN EXCHANGE, AND 2) EITHER: • DEBTOR'S REMAINING ASSETS WERE UNREASONABLY SMALL IN RELATION TO BUSINESS OR TRANSACTION, OR • DEBTOR INTENDED TO INCUR OR BELIEVED WOULD INCUR DEBTS BEYOND ABILITY TO PAY	1) DEBTOR RECEIVED LESS THAN A REASONABLY EQUIVALENT VALUE IN EXCHANGE, AND 2) DEBTOR WAS INSOLVENT OR WAS RENDERED INSOLVENT	TRANSFER TO INSIDER FOR ANTECEDENT DEBT IF: 1) DEBTOR WAS INSOLVENT AT TIME, AND 2) INSIDER HAD REASONABLE CAUSE TO BELIEVE DEBTOR WAS INSOLVENT

4. Preference

Section 547 of the Bankruptcy Code is designed to discourage creditors from exerting pressure on a troubled debtor to obtain transfers of property (whether in the form of payments or the creation of a security interest or otherwise) when that property is needed to maximize the likelihood of the debtor's financial survival. It does so by creating a time period prior to bankruptcy—90 days for most creditors and one year for "insiders," Section 101(31), of the debtor—during which a "transfer," Section 101(54), of an interest in the debtor's property may be avoidable by the trustee in bankruptcy. The requirements for avoidance of a preferential transfer are visualized below.

PREFERENTIAL TRANSFER
§ 547(b)

TRANSFER OF AN INTEREST OF DEBTOR IN PROPERTY

1) TO OR FOR THE BENEFIT OF CREDITOR

2) FOR OR ON ACCOUNT OF ANTECEDENT DEBT

3) MADE WHILE DEBTOR WAS INSOLVENT

4) MADE DURING PREFERENCE PERIOD

- WITHIN 90 DAYS PRIOR TO BANKRUPTCY FOR NON-INSIDERS

- WITHIN ONE YEAR PRIOR TO BANKRUPTCY FOR INSIDERS

5) PREFERENTIAL EFFECT = CREDITOR RECEIVES MORE THAN CREDITOR WOULD RECEIVE IF:

- CASE WERE CHAPTER 7,

- TRANSFER HAD NOT BEEN MADE, AND

- CREDITOR RECEIVED PAYMENT IN LIQUIDATION

Under Section 547(f), the debtor is presumed to have been insolvent during the 90 days immediately preceding the date of the filing of the bankruptcy petition. Therefore, the trustee in bankruptcy does not have to prove insolvency in the case of a transfer to a non-insider.

Although determining the time a transfer is made is relatively easy when property physically moves from one party to another, the timing of a transfer consisting of a security interest is more problematic. Section 547(e)(2) provides rules for establishing when a transfer of a security interest is made depending on when the security interest is perfected. A visualization of the rules follows:

TIME OF TRANSFER OF SECURITY INTEREST § 547(e)(2)		
PERFECTED AT TIME OF ATTACHMENT OR WITHIN 30 DAYS THEREAFTER	PERFECTED LATER THAN 30 DAYS AFTER ATTACHMENT	NEVER PERFECTED
TRANSFER OCCURS AT TIME OF ATTACHMENT § 547(e)(2)(A)	TRANSFER OCCURS AT TIME OF PERFECTION § 547(e)(2)(B)	TRANSFER OCCURS IMMEDIATELY PRIOR TO BANKRUPTCY § 547(e)(2)(C)

Under Section 547(e)(3), a transfer is not made until the debtor has acquired rights in the property transferred. Therefore, a security interest that attaches to after-acquired property is not a "transfer" until the debtor has rights to that property, and if those rights are acquired within the preference period, the transfer may be a preference.

The broad definition of a preferential transfer in Section 547(b) captures many transactions that are beneficial to a financially-troubled debtor and that should not be disrupted by the trustee after the fact merely because the debtor is in bankruptcy. There are nine exceptions to the preference avoiding power of the trustee listed in Section 547(c). We will focus on the first five as having the most relevance to a secured creditor.

A visualization of the exceptions to the trustee's power to avoid preferences follows:

EXCEPTIONS TO PREFERENCES § 547(c)
1) SUBSTANTIALLY CONTEMPORANEOUS EXCHANGE FOR NEW VALUE
2) ORDINARY COURSE OF BUSINESS PAYMENTS
3) PMSI
4) NEW VALUE TEST
5) NET IMPROVEMENT IN POSITION TEST (FLOATING LIEN)
6) STATUTORY LIENS
7) DOMESTIC SUPPORT OBLIGATIONS
8) SMALL CONSUMER TRANSFERS < $600
9) SMALL NON-CONSUMER TRANSFERS < $5,000

The first exception to the trustee's power to avoid preferential transfers is for transfers for contemporaneous exchanges for new value. This would include, for example, a transfer of a security interest in exchange for a release of previously-held collateral, or in exchange for a new extension of credit. There are two requirements to satisfy this exception. A visualization of the exception follows:

SUBSTANTIALLY CONTEMPORANEOUS EXCHANGE FOR NEW VALUE § 547(c)(1)
TRANSFER WAS:
1) INTENDED BY DEBTOR AND CREDITOR TO BE CONTEMPORANEOUS EXCHANGE FOR NEW VALUE, AND
2) IN FACT SUBSTANTIALLY CONTEMPORANEOUS EXCHANGE

The second exception protects transfers that constitute payments in the ordinary course of business. This exception protects regularly scheduled payments on secured debt, as well as other ordinary course payments. There are two requirements for the exception. One looks at the nature of the debt in respect of which the payment is made. The other focuses on the nature of the payment. A visualization of the exception follows:

ORDINARY COURSE OF BUSINESS PAYMENTS
§ 547(c)(2)

1) DEBT INCURRED IN ORDINARY COURSE OF BUSINESS OF BOTH PARTIES, AND

2) EITHER

- PAYMENT MADE IN ORDINARY COURSE OF BUSINESS OF BOTH PARTIES, OR

- PAYMENT MADE ACCORDING TO ORDINARY BUSINESS TERMS

The third exception is often called the PMSI exception, because it protects perfected purchase-money security interests. Unlike UCC § 9-317, the Bankruptcy Code protects a PMSI from attack by the trustee in bankruptcy as a preference if it is perfected within 30 days (rather than 20) after the debtor receives possession of the collateral. A visualization of the exception follows:

PMSI EXCEPTION
§ 547(c)(3)

---

1) SECURITY INTEREST SECURES NEW VALUE:

- GIVEN AT OR AFTER SIGNING OF SECURITY AGREEMENT DESCRIBING COLLATERAL,
- GIVEN BY OR ON BEHALF OF SECURED PARTY,
- GIVEN TO ENABLE DEBTOR TO ACQUIRE COLLATERAL, AND
- IN FACT USED TO ACQUIRE COLLATERAL

AND

2) SECURITY INTEREST PERFECTED WITHIN 30 DAYS AFTER DEBTOR RECEIVES POSSESSION OF COLLATERAL

The fourth exception protects creditors to the extent that, after receiving a preferential transfer, they return an equivalent value to the debtor on an unsecured basis which remains in the estate. A visualization of the exception follows:

NEW VALUE TEST
§ 547(c)(4)

---

1) PREFERENTIAL TRANSFER FROM DEBTOR TO CREDITOR,

2) LATER NEW VALUE GIVEN BY CREDITOR TO DEBTOR, AND

3) DEBTOR DOES NOT GIVE UNAVOIDABLE SECURITY INTEREST OR MAKE UNAVOIDABLE TRANSFER TO CREDITOR ON ACCOUNT OF NEW VALUE

The final exception that may be of relevance to a secured creditor is sometimes called the two-point net improvement test. As we already saw, Section 547(e)(3) specifically states that a transfer is not made until the debtor has acquired rights in the property transferred. This provision makes the secured creditor's interest in all collateral in which a secured creditor obtains a security interest under an after-acquired property clause subject to avoidance as a preferential transfer.

That result may be a risk some creditors may be willing to take. For example, if a creditor takes a security interest in equipment, the inability of the creditor to be sure that the security interest will be unavoidable to the extent it attaches to after-acquired equipment may be unimportant as long as the equipment that exists at the time the loan is made is likely to be in the debtor's possession at the time of bankruptcy. However, creditors who lend against inventory and accounts, which in the ordinary course of business disappear (by sale and by collection) and are replaced by new inventory and accounts, would not be willing to engage in these financing transactions if they knew that the security interest in the after-acquired collateral would be avoidable in its entirety with respect to collateral acquired within 90 days of bankruptcy.

To meet the concerns of the financing industry, Congress included an exception to the trustee's power to avoid preferential transfers for perfected security interests in inventory or accounts (or their proceeds) to the extent that the secured creditor does not improve its position (that is, the extent to which its claim is collateralized) during the applicable preference period. A visualization of the exception follows:

TWO-POINT NET IMPROVEMENT EXCEPTION § 547(c)(5)	
EXCEPTION	**EXCEPTION TO EXCEPTION**
TRANSFER THAT CREATES PERFECTED SECURITY INTEREST IN INVENTORY, RECEIVABLES AND/OR PROCEEDS	CAN AVOID TRANSFER TO EXTENT THAT AGGREGATE TRANSFERS TO TRANSFEREE DURING APPLICABLE PREFERENCE PERIOD (90 DAYS OR 1 YEAR) REDUCED AMOUNT BY WHICH SECURED DEBT EXCEEDED VALUE OF COLLATERAL

As you think about the two-point net improvement exception, you will realize that there are four possible scenarios to which it can be applied. If the value of the collateral at least equals to amount of the secured claim at the beginning of the preference period (no deficiency in collateral value), at the time of the bankruptcy filing the value of the collateral can either (1) at least equal the amount of the secured claim (no deficiency), or (2) be less than the amount of the secured claim (deficiency in collateral value). In either of these two situations, Section 547(c)(5) would protect the secured creditor from preference attack because the secured creditor has not improved its position during the preference period. A creditor who is fully-secured by its inventory and accounts collateral at the beginning of the preference period will never be subject to preference attack for its after-acquired inventory or accounts or proceeds.

If, however, the value of the collateral is less than the amount of the secured claim at the beginning of the preference period (so that there is a deficiency between the value of the collateral and the amount of the claim, *i.e.*, the secured creditor is under-secured), at the time of the bankruptcy filing the value of the collateral can either (1) at least equal the amount of the secured claim (no deficiency), or (2) be less than the amount of the secured claim (still a deficiency). In the first of these two situations, the secured creditor has clearly received a preference to the extent that its claim has changed from under-secured to fully-secured, and the trustee may avoid the security interest in the after-acquired collateral to the extent of that improvement. In the second situation, the secured creditor was under-secured at the beginning of the preference period, and is still under-secured, but if the secured creditor is LESS under-secured, the trustee may avoid the security interest to the extent of the improvement in position. If the secured creditor is MORE under-secured, there is no improvement and no preference. A visualization of the four scenarios follows:

TWO-POINT NET IMPROVEMENT SCENARIOS § 547(c)(5)		
	NO DEFICIENCY AT BANKRUPTCY	DEFICIENCY AT BANKRUPTCY
NO DEFICIENCY AT START OF PREFERENCE PERIOD	NO PREFERENCE (NO IMPROVEMENT IN POSITION)	NO PREFERENCE (NO IMPROVEMENT IN POSITION)
DEFICIENCY AT START OF PREFERENCE PERIOD	PREFERENCE (IMPROVEMENT IN POSITION)	1) DEFICIENCY IS GREATER AT START OF PREFERENCE PERIOD = PREFERENCE (IMPROVEMENT IN POSITION) 2) DEFICIENCY IS GREATER AT BANKRUPTCY = NO PREFERENCE (NO IMPROVEMENT IN POSITION)

F. TREATMENT OF SECURED CLAIM

The goal of a bankruptcy case for most debtors is to obtain a discharge of prepetition debts. The Bankruptcy Code provides for the discharge of debts, but does not discharge security interests. Therefore, except as otherwise provided under the Bankruptcy Code, a security interest remains effective with respect to the collateral during and after a bankruptcy case of the debtor.

We have already discussed the impact of the automatic stay on the secured creditor, and the protections afforded to the secured creditor if the debtor wishes to use, lease or dispose of the collateral. We will not look at what the secured creditor will receive in respect of its secured claim during the debtor's bankruptcy case.

1. Chapter 7

In a chapter 7 case, all non-exempt property of the debtor will be liquidated by the trustee in bankruptcy, and the proceeds will be distributed to creditors pro rata in accordance with their respective priorities. Before final distribution of property of the estate, the trustee in bankruptcy is directed to dispose of any property in which an entity other than the estate as an interest, such as a lien. Section 725. It may dispose of collateral by abandoning it to the secured party pursuant to Section 554, or may sell it pursuant to Section 363 and provide the proceeds to the secured party.

All exempt property claimed by an individual debtor will be turned over to the debtor by the trustee, but it remains subject to any prepetition security interest and the secured creditor retains the right to exercise remedies with respect to that security interest, discussed in Chapter 11, after the bankruptcy case is concluded.

If a debtor wishes to retain the collateral without risking the exercise of remedies by the secured creditor, it has two options. First, in the case of tangible personal property intended primarily for personal, family, or household use, an individual debtor may redeem the collateral under Section 722 by paying the secured creditor the full amount of the allowed secured claim. The right to redeem collateral cannot be waived, and does not require consent by the secured party. A visualization of Section 722 follows:

TYPE OF DEBTOR	TYPE OF DEBT	REDEMPTION § 722 TYPE OF PROPERTY	TREATMENT OF PROPERTY IN BANKRUPTCY	PAYMENT TO SECURED CREDITOR
INDIVIDUAL	DISCHARGEABLE CONSUMER DEBT	TANGIBLE PERSONAL PROPERTY INTENDED PRIMARILY FOR PERSONAL, FAMILY, OR HOUSEHOLD USE	1) CLAIMED AS EXEMPT UNDER § 522 2) ABANDONED BY TRUSTEE UNDER § 554	AMOUNT OF ALLOWED SECURED CLAIM IN FULL AT TIME OF REDEMPTION

The second means by which a debtor may retain property in which a secured creditor has a security interest is by entering into a valid reaffirmation agreement with respect to the secured debt under Section 524(c). A reaffirmation agreement is an agreement under which a debtor agrees to be liable for (reaffirms) a debt that would otherwise be dischargeable in the bankruptcy case. Although a reaffirmation agreement may be negotiated with respect to any debt, it is most likely to be entered into by a debtor with respect to debt secured by collateral the debtor is unable to redeem but wishes to retain. A debtor may enter into a reaffirmation agreement only with the concurrence of the creditor, and the terms of that agreement are subject to negotiation. A visualization of the requirements for a valid reaffirmation agreement under Section 524(c) follows:

REAFFIRMATION AGREEMENT § 524(c)				
TIMING	DISCLOSURES	FILING WITH COURT	COURT APPROVAL	ABILITY TO RESCIND
AGREEMENT IS MADE PRIOR TO DISCHARGE	DEBTOR RECEIVED § 524(k) DISCLOSURES BEFORE SIGNING	AGREEMENT IS FILED AND, IF DEBTOR WAS REPRESENTED BY COUNSEL, COUNSEL FILED AFFIDAVIT THAT: 1) AGREEMENT REPRESENTS FULLY INFORMED AND VOLUNTARY AGREEMENT, 2) AGREEMENT DOES NOT IMPOSE UNDUE HARDSHIP, AND 3) COUNSEL ADVISED DEBTOR OF LEGAL EFFECT AND CONSEQUENCES OF AGREEMENT AND DEFAULT	IF INDIVIDUAL DEBTOR WAS NOT REPRESENTED BY COUNSEL, COURT APPROVES AGREEMENT AS: 1) NOT IMPOSING UNDUE HARDSHIP, AND 2) IN THE BEST INTEREST OF DEBTOR	DEBTOR MAY RESCIND AGREEMENT AT ANY TIME PRIOR TO LATER OF: 1) DISCHARGE, AND 2) 60 DAYS AFTER AGREEMENT FILED WITH COURT

An individual debtor in a chapter 7 case must file with the clerk within 30 days after the filing of the petition a statement of intention with respect to the retention or surrender of collateral and, if applicable, specifying whether the collateral is claimed as exempt, that the debtor intends to redeem the collateral, or that the debtor intends to reaffirm the debts secured by such collateral. Section 521(a)(2)(A). The debtor must perform the intention expressed by that statement within 30 days after the first date set for a meeting of creditors under Section 341(a), unless the court, for cause, provides extra time. Section 521(a)(2)(B). The individual debtor may not retain personal property in which a creditor has a purchase-money security interest unless the debtor redeems the property or reaffirms the debt within 45 days after the first meeting of creditors under Section 341(a), or the automatic stay is terminated with respect to that property unless the court orders otherwise and orders adequate protection to the creditor. Section 521(a)(6).

2. Chapter 13

Chapter 13, which allows an "individual with regular income," Section 101(30), to obtain a discharge of prepetition debts by making payments to creditors out of the debtor's future income under a plan, provides the debtor more flexibility in dealing with his or her secured debt. Under Section 1322(b), a chapter 13 plan may provide for modification of secured debt, curing or waiving any default, or curing defaults and maintaining payments on debt whose maturity is later than the end of the chapter 13 plan. A visualization of the options afforded by Section 1322(b) follows:

CHAPTER 13 PLAN
TREATMENT OF DEBT SECURED BY PERSONAL PROPERTY
§ 1322(b)

1) MODIFY OR LEAVE UNAFFECTED RIGHTS OF HOLDERS OF CLAIMS,

2) PROVIDE FOR CURING OR WAIVING OF ANY DEFAULT, AND/OR

3) IF LAST PAYMENT IS DUE AFTER DATE OF FINAL PAYMENT UNDER PLAN, PROVIDE FOR CURING OF ANY DEFAULT WITHIN REASONABLE TIME, AND MAINTENANCE OF PAYMENTS DURING CASE

The confirmation requirements for a chapter 13 plan set forth in Section 1325 impose limitations on the extent to which a secured claim may be modified under Section 1322(b). Section 1325(a)(5) provides that a chapter 13 plan must deal with secured debts in one of three ways before a court may confirm the plan. One is for the secured creditor to accept the plan (and therefore approve of its treatment). Another is for the debtor to surrender the collateral to the secured creditor. The final way is for the plan to provide for the secured creditor to retain its lien and for property to be distributed to the secured creditor having a value, as of the effective date of the plan, of not less that the allowed amount of the claim.

A visualization of the confirmation requirements for a chapter 13 plan with respect to secured claims follows:

CHAPTER 13 PLAN CONFIRMATION REQUIREMENTS FOR SECURED CLAIMS § 1325(a)(5)		
SECURED CREDITOR ACCEPTS PLAN, OR	PLAN PROVIDES THAT: • SECURED CREDITOR RETAINS LIEN, AND • PROPERTY DISTRIBUTED TO SECURED CREDITOR HAVING VALUE AS OF EFFECTIVE DATE OF PLAN OF NOT LESS THAN ALLOWED AMOUNT OF CLAIM, OR	DEBTOR SURRENDERS COLLATERAL TO SECURED CREDITOR

3. Chapter 11

Under Chapter 11, a debtor satisfies its prepetition debts in accordance with a plan of reorganization. The plan of reorganization has few constraints on its contents. Under Section 1123, it may impair or leave unimpaired (see Section 1124 for a discussion of impairment) any class of claims, secured or unsecured. Section 1123(b)(1). It may also modify the rights of secured creditors or leave unaffected those rights. Section 1123(b)(5).

As was true in chapter 13, the constraints on the ability of the debtor to modify or impair a secured claim are contained in the confirmation requirements for the chapter 11 plan, in Section 1129. Several of those provisions protect the secured creditor. First, if the secured claim is impaired, the secured creditor must either accept the plan or receive under the plan property with a value, as of the effective date of the plan, not less than the amount the secured creditor would receive if the debtor were liquidated under chapter 7 on that date. Section 1129(a)(7). This is called the "best interests" test, and protects each creditor from being forced to receive less in chapter 11 than it would in a chapter 7 liquidation.

Second, confirmation of a plan generally requires the acceptance of the plan by each impaired class of claims. Section 1129(a)(8). In most cases, a secured creditor is placed in its own "class," see Section 1122 on classification, and therefore must vote to approve the plan. However, even if the secured creditor votes against the plan, the plan may still be confirmed if there is one class of impaired claims that votes to accept the plan, and the debtor requests the court to confirm the plan over the objection of the secured creditor. This is called a "cramdown" plan. Section 1129(b).

But the secured creditor is also given special protections if confirmation of a cramdown plan is sought. A cramdown plan can be confirmed over the objection of a secured creditor only if it "does not discriminate unfairly, and is fair and equitable" with respect to the secured creditor. The requirement that the plan be "fair and equitable" to a class of secured claims mandates that the class be treated in one of three ways under Section 1129(b)(2)(A). One is for the secured creditor to retain its lien and receive deferred cash payments totaling at least the allowed amount of the claim and having a value as of the effective date of the plan of at least the value of the collateral. Another is for the collateral to be sold and the security interest to attach to the proceeds (which would then be treated consistent with one of the other options). Finally, the secured creditor may be given the "indubitable equivalent" of its secured claim, as determined by the court.

Confirmation of a chapter 11 plan of reorganization binds a secured creditor whether or not its claim is impaired, and whether or not it voted to accept the plan. Section 1141(a).

A visualization of the cramdown requirements for secured creditors follows:

CRAMDOWN OF SECURED CLAIMS § 1129(b)			
	REQUIREMENTS FOR CRAMDOWN § 1129(b)(1)		"FAIR AND EQUITABLE" § 1129(b)(2)(A)
1)	ALL REQUIREMENTS FOR CONFIRMATION MET EXCEPT UNANIMOUS APPROVAL,	1)	SECURED PARTY RETAINS LIEN AND RECEIVES DEFERRED CASH • AT LEAST EQUAL TO ALLOWED AMOUNT OF CLAIM, AND • HAVING PRESENT VALUE AT LEAST EQUAL TO VALUE OF COLLATERAL, OR
2)	REQUEST BY PLAN PROPONENT FOR CRAMDOWN,		
3)	PLAN IS "FAIR AND EQUITABLE," AND		
4)	PLAN "DOES NOT DISCRIMINATE UNFAIRLY"		
		2)	PROPERTY SOLD AND LIEN ATTACHES TO PROCEEDS, OR
		3)	INDUBITABLE EQUIVALENT OF CLAIM

Chapter 8
DISPOSITION OF COLLATERAL AND PROCEEDS

We already looked at the general priority rules allowing certain buyers of collateral to take free of security interests. In some cases, secured creditors expect that their collateral will be disposed of by the debtor in the ordinary course of business. For example, a debtor in the retail industry will not thrive unless its inventory is sold to buyers. In other cases, secured creditors may take a security interest in collateral that it anticipates will be sold, even if that transaction is not in the ordinary course of business. For example, the security interest may be in a piece of equipment that the debtor intends to sell in order to acquire more modern equipment.

If the secured party authorizes the sale of collateral free and clear of its security interest, the secured interest is removed from the collateral upon its disposition. However, if the debtor disposes of the collateral without authorization from the secured party, the person acquiring the collateral takes it subject to the security interest unless the acquiror can invoke a rule of priority allowing it to prevail. § 9-315(a)(1).

In either case (that is, in the case of a sale that is authorized by the secured party or one that is not), the debtor is likely to receive something in exchange for the disposition, such as money, or an account, or chattel paper, or an instrument, or another type of property. Under § 9-315(a)(2), a security interest in collateral automatically attaches to any "identifiable proceeds" of that collateral. This means that if the sale was authorized free and clear of the security interest in the collateral, the secured creditor substitutes for its security interest in the collateral a security interest in the identifiable proceeds of that collateral. If the sale was unauthorized, the secured creditor retains its security interest in the collateral in the hands of the acquiror of the collateral, and also gets a security interest in the identifiable proceeds of the disposition.

A visualization of the position of the secured party upon disposition of the collateral follows:

IMPACT OF DISPOSITION OF COLLATERAL UPON SECURITY INTEREST § 9-315(a)	
AUTHORIZED DISPOSITIONS	UNAUTHORIZED DISPOSITIONS
SECURED PARTY HAS SECURITY INTEREST IN: IDENTIFIABLE PROCEEDS	SECURED PARTY HAS SECURITY INTEREST IN: COLLATERAL IN HANDS OF ACQUIROR, AND IDENTIFIABLE PROCEEDS

It should be noted that if the acquiror of the collateral takes it subject to the security interest, a secured creditor of the acquiror who acquires a security interest in the newly-acquired property will be subordinate to the security interest created by the first debtor, even if that second secured creditor was the first to file under the general rules of priority. § 9-325. There are special rules to resolve priority disputes when the acquiror becomes a "new debtor," § 9-102(a)(56), with respect to an existing security interest in collateral. *See* § 9-326.

What are "identifiable proceeds"? "Proceeds" is defined in § 9-102(a)(64). They include not only "whatever is acquired upon the sale, lease, license, exchange, or other disposition of collateral," but also other property, rights or claims arising out of the collateral. A visualization of the definition of "proceeds" follows:

PROCEEDS § 9-102(a)(64)	
1)	WHATEVER IS ACQUIRED UPON DISPOSITION OF COLLATERAL,
2)	WHATEVER IS COLLECTED ON OR DISTRIBUTED ON ACCOUNT OF COLLATERAL,
3)	RIGHTS ARISING OUT OF COLLATERAL,
4)	CLAIMS ARISING OUT OF LOSS, NONCONFORMITY, INTERFERENCE WITH USE OF, DEFECTS, INFRINGEMENT OR DAMAGE TO COLLATERAL UP TO VALUE THEREOF, OR
5)	INSURANCE PAYABLE FOR LOSS, NONCONFORMITY, DEFECTS, INFRINGEMENT OR DAMAGE TO COLLATERAL UP TO VALUE THEREOF

Proceeds are always identifiable when they are not commingled with other property. When they are commingled, § 9-315(b) provides that they constitute "identifiable" proceeds under two circumstances. If the proceeds are goods and the goods are commingled, § 9-336 describes the extent to which a security interest attaches to them. See discussion of commingled goods in Chapter 6. If the proceeds are not goods, they are identifiable "to the extent that the secured party identifies the proceeds by a method of tracing, including application of equitable principles, that is permitted under" non-Article 9 law with respect to that type of property.

The problem of commingled proceeds frequently arises in the context of deposit accounts into which both proceeds and non-proceeds have been deposited, and from which withdrawals have been made. Official Comment 3 to § 9-315 directs us that an appropriate reference to resolve such problems is the "lowest intermediate balance rule" discussed in Restatement (2d) of Trusts § 202. Under the lowest intermediate balance rule (sometimes abbreviated as LIBR), deposits of proceeds into a deposit account are deemed to increase the identifiable proceeds in the account. Deposits of non-proceeds, unless the deposits are explicitly intended to replenish proceeds previously withdrawn, do not increase identifiable proceeds in the deposit account. When a withdrawal is made from the deposit account, it will be deemed to come from funds in the account that do not constitute proceeds of collateral until there are no non-proceeds remaining. From that point on, withdrawals are deemed to come from identifiable proceeds.

A visualization of the lowest intermediate balance rule follows:

LOWEST INTERMEDIATE BALANCE RULE			
DEPOSITS		WITHDRAWALS	
PROCEEDS	NON-PROCEEDS	1)	FIRST, FROM NON-PROCEEDS UNTIL THERE ARE NONE LEFT
INCREASE IDENTIFIABLE PROCEEDS	DO NOT INCREASE IDENTIFIABLE PROCEEDS UNLESS INTENT TO MAKE RESTITUTION FOR PRIOR WITHDRAWAL OF PROCEEDS	2)	THEN, FROM PROCEEDS

As we previously discussed, a security interest in collateral automatically attaches to any identifiable proceeds of collateral under § 9-315(a)(2). However, if the debtor files for bankruptcy protection, the court has the power under § 552 of the Bankruptcy Code to limit or remove the security interest in proceeds "based on the equities of the case." See discussion of postpetition effect of security interest in Chapter 7.

A secured creditor, of course, wants a security interest that not only attaches to proceeds but is perfected as well. Section 9-315 also addresses this concern. Under § 9-315(c), a security interest in proceeds is automatically perfected if the security interest in the collateral giving rise to the proceeds was perfected. This perfection generally ceases 20 days after the security interest attaches to the proceeds unless the secured creditor has taken or takes action to perfect by other means before the end of that period. § 9-315(d).

There are two situations in which the automatic perfection continues beyond the 20-day period without further action by the secured creditor. The first is for "identifiable cash proceeds." § 9-315(d)(2). We have already looked at the concept of "identifiable" proceeds. "Cash proceeds" are defined in § 9-102(a)(9) as proceeds that are "money, checks, deposit accounts, or the like." All other proceeds are "noncash proceeds." § 9-102(a)(58). Therefore, if the proceeds of the collateral are cash proceeds that are not commingled or, if commingled, can be identified by a method of tracing (such as the lowest intermediate balance rule), the security interest automatically attaches to those proceeds, is automatically perfected, and remains perfected beyond 20 days without further action by the secured party.

The other situation in which a security interest in proceeds remains perfected beyond the 20-day period of automatic perfection given by § 9-315(c) and (d) is when three conditions are met. First, there is a filed financing statement covering the original collateral. Second, the proceeds are a type of collateral as to which one could perfect a security interest by filing a financing statement in the same location as that filed financing statement. Third, the proceeds must not be acquired with cash proceeds (that is, they are not "second generation" proceeds acquired with cash proceeds). In this situation, the security interest remains perfected at least for the 20-day automatic perfection period, and beyond that period until the filed financing statement covering the original collateral is no longer effective.

A visualization of the rules of § 9-315 on perfection of security interests in proceeds follows:

PERFECTION OF SECURITY INTEREST IN PROCEEDS § 9-315			
AUTOMATIC PERFECTION	DURATION OF AUTOMATIC PERFECTION		
	RULE	EXCEPTIONS	
IF SECURITY INTEREST IN ORIGINAL COLLATERAL IS PERFECTED, SECURITY INTEREST IN PROCEEDS IS AUTOMATICALLY PERFECTED § 9-315(c)	PERFECTION CEASES 21st DAY AFTER ATTACHMENT UNLESS PERFECTION OCCURS BY OTHER MEANS § 9-315(d)(3)	IDENTIFIABLE CASH PROCEEDS PERFECTION CONTINUES INDEFINITELY § 9-315(d)(2)	OTHER PROCEEDS IF: 1) FILED FINANCING STATEMENT COVERS ORIGINAL COLLATERAL, 2) SECURITY INTEREST IN PROCEEDS CAN BE PERFECTED BY FILING IN SAME LOCATION, AND 3) PROCEEDS ARE NOT ACQUIRED WITH CASH PROCEEDS THEN: PERFECTION CONTINUES UNTIL LATER OF 21st DAY AFTER ATTACHMENT AND DATE FILING BECOMES INEFFECTIVE § 9-315(d)(1) & § 9-315(e)

A perfected security interest in proceeds enjoys the same advantages with respect to the general priority rules as the security interest in the collateral from which it springs. The basic priority rules are discussed in Chapter 6. Therefore, if a perfected security interest in proceeds is competing with an unperfected security interest in the same proceeds, the perfected security interest will prevail. § 9-322(a)(2). If the perfected security interest in proceeds is competing with another perfected security interest in the same proceeds, the first to file or perfected will prevails. § 9-322(a)(1). In determining the time of filing or perfection as to a security interest in proceeds, § 9-322(b)(1) tells us that the time of filing or perfection as to the security interest in the original collateral is also the time of filing or perfection as to the security interest in the proceeds generated by that collateral. If the perfected security interest is competing with a lien creditor, the perfected security interest prevails. § 9-317(a)(1).

If a security interest in proceeds is not perfected, it will lose to a competing perfected security interest in the proceeds. § 9-322(a)(2). If it is competing with another unperfected security interest in proceeds, the first to attach or become effective will prevail. § 9-322(a)(3). If it is competing with a lien creditor, the unperfected security interest will prevail if a financing statement has been filed and one of the conditions specified in § 9-203(b)(3) is met before the lien creditor has an interest in the proceeds. § 9-317(a)(2).

A visualization of the general priority rules for proceeds follows:

GENERAL PRIORITY RULES FOR PROCEEDS		
	PERFECTED SECURITY INTEREST IN PROCEEDS	UNPERFECTED SECURITY INTEREST IN PROCEEDS
PERFECTED SECURITY INTEREST IN PROCEEDS	FIRST TO FILE OR PERFECT PREVAILS, WITH TIME OF FILING OR PERFECTION AS TO PROCEEDS BEING TIME OF FILING OR PERFECTION AS TO COLLATERAL § 9-322(a)(1) & § 9-322(b)(1)	PERFECTED SECURITY INTEREST PREVAILS § 9-322(a)(2)
UNPERFECTED SECURITY INTEREST IN PROCEEDS	PERFECTED SECURITY INTEREST PREVAILS § 9-322(a)(2)	FIRST TO ATTACH OR BECOME EFFECTIVE PREVAILS § 9-322(a)(3)
LIEN CREDITOR	PERFECTED SECURITY INTEREST PREVAILS § 9-317(a)(1)	UNPERFECTED SECURITY INTEREST PREVAILS IF 1) FILED FINANCING STATEMENT, AND 2) ONE OF CONDITIONS IN § 9-203(b)(3) SATISFIED BEFORE LIEN ARISES

The basic priority rules with respect to buyers, lessees and licensees, also discussed in Chapter 6, apply to security interests in proceeds to the same extent as other security interests.

As was true for security interests in collateral generally, security interests in proceeds also have some special priority rules that override the general priority rules for certain types of transactions or certain types of collateral. The first is for the purchase-money security interest. You recall that the holder of a purchase-money security interest is able to obtain priority over competing security interests under the circumstances described in § 9-324. That section also specifies the extent to which the PMSI holder is able to extend its priority to proceeds of the collateral in which it has the PMSI. For non-inventory collateral, the PMSI priority extends to perfected security interests in identifiable proceeds of the collateral. For inventory, the PMSI priority extends to identifiable cash proceeds received on or before the delivery of the inventory to a buyer, and to proceeds received upon disposition of the inventory in the form of chattel paper or instruments to the extent provided by the special priority rules of § 9-330. The holder of the inventory PMSI does not get special priority for any other proceeds received upon its disposition.

A visualization of the special priority rules for proceeds of a PMSI follows:

PRIORITY FOR PROCEEDS OF PMSI § 9-324	
NON-INVENTORY § 9-324(a)	INVENTORY § 9-324(b)
PRIORITY FOR PMSI EXTENDS TO PERFECTED SECURITY INTEREST IN IDENTIFIABLE PROCEEDS	PRIORITY FOR PMSI EXTENDS TO PERFECTED SECURITY INTEREST IN PROCEEDS CONSTITUTING 1) CHATTEL PAPER AND PROCEEDS OF CHATTEL PAPER TO EXTENT PROVIDED IN § 9-330 2) INSTRUMENT TO EXTENT PROVIDED IN § 9-330 3) IDENTIFIABLE CASH PROCEEDS RECEIVED ON OR BEFORE THE DELIVERY OF THE INVENTORY TO A BUYER

The second category of special priority rules for proceeds relates to proceeds of certain types of collateral as to which a secured creditor may perfect a method other than filing (what the drafters of Article 9 call "non-filing collateral"). The special priority rules relating to this deposit accounts (§ 9-327), investment property (§ 9-328), letter-of-credit rights (§ 9-329), chattel paper (§ 9-330) and instruments (§ 9-330) were discussed in Chapter 6. Section 9-322(c)(2) tells us that these special priority rules extend to proceeds of these types of collateral if three conditions are satisfied. A visualization of the requirements for obtaining special priority for proceeds of non-filing collateral follows:

```
┌─────────────────────────────────────────────────────────────────┐
│                                                                 │
│        SPECIAL PRIORITY RULES FOR NON-FILING PROCEEDS           │
│                  OF NON-FILING COLLATERAL                       │
│                       § 9-322(c)(2)                             │
│                                                                 │
├─────────────────────────────────────────────────────────────────┤
│                                                                 │
│  IF SECURITY INTEREST IN COLLATERAL HAS PRIORITY UNDER          │
│  §§ 9-327 – 9-331, SECURITY INTEREST IN PROCEEDS ALSO HAS       │
│  PRIORITY IF:                                                   │
│                                                                 │
│  1)   SECURITY INTEREST IN PROCEEDS IS PERFECTED,               │
│                                                                 │
│  2)   PROCEEDS ARE CASH PROCEEDS OR OF SAME TYPE AS COLLATERAL, │
│       AND                                                       │
│                                                                 │
│  3)   FOR PROCEEDS OF PROCEEDS, ALL INTERVENING PROCEEDS ARE    │
│       CASH PROCEEDS, SAME TYPE AS COLLATERAL OR ACCOUNT         │
│                                                                 │
└─────────────────────────────────────────────────────────────────┘
```

The final special priority rule in § 9-322 also relates to non-filing collateral. Section 9-322(d) and (e) state that, if a security interest in chattel paper, deposit accounts, negotiable documents, instruments, investment property or letter-of-credit rights is perfected other than by filing, conflicting security interests in proceeds of that collateral of the type as to which one files to perfect a security interest (*i.e.*, not cash proceeds, chattel paper, negotiable documents, instruments, investment property, or letter-of-credit rights) rank according to priority in time of filing. A visualization of this special priority rule follows:

SPECIAL PRIORITY RULE FOR FILING PROCEEDS OF NON-FILING COLLATERAL § 9-322(d) & (e)		
TYPE OF COLLATERAL	TYPE OF PROCEEDS	RULE
CHATTEL PAPER DEPOSIT ACCOUNTS NEGOTIABLE DOCUMENTS INSTRUMENTS INVESTMENT PROPERTY LETTER-OF-CREDIT RIGHTS	*NOT*: CASH PROCEEDS CHATTEL PAPER NEGOTIABLE DOCUMENTS INSTRUMENTS INVESTMENT PROPERTY LETTER-OF-CREDIT RIGHTS	IF SECURITY INTEREST IN COLLATERAL IS PERFECTED OTHER THAN BY FILING, FIRST TO FILE AS TO PROCEEDS PREVAILS

Chapter 9
RIGHTS AND DUTIES OF SECURED PARTY

By virtue of taking a security interest in collateral, a secured party undertakes certain limited duties to the debtor. The first set of duties arises if the secured party takes possession or control of collateral. Under § 9-207(a), the secured party is required to use reasonable care in the custody and preservation of collateral in its possession. (This duty does not apply to a secured party who buys accounts, chattel paper, payments intangibles, or promissory notes or to a consignor unless the secured party is entitled to charge back against uncollected collateral or otherwise to full or limited recourse based on nonpayment.) The duty of care may not be disclaimed by agreement, but the parties may contractually agree to the standards by which it may be judged, so long as those standards are not manifestly unreasonable. § 1-302(b).

It should be noted that the mere existence of a security interest or agricultural lien, or the fact that the debtor is able to use or dispose of collateral, does not impose any liability on the secured party for the debtor's acts or omissions, either as a matter of contract or tort. § 9-402.

Section 9-207 also sets forth certain other duties of the secured party, as well as certain rights of the secured party with respect to collateral in its possession or control, and the continuing responsibilities of the debtor. A visualization of these rights and duties follows:

RIGHTS AND DUTIES FOR COLLATERAL IN POSSESSION OR CONTROL OF SECURED PARTY § 9-207		
DUTIES OF SECURED PARTY	**RIGHTS OF SECURED PARTY**	**DUTIES OF DEBTOR**
1) MUST USE REASONABLE CARE IN CUSTODY AND PRESERVATION OF COLLATERAL IN ITS POSSESSION, 2) MUST KEEP NON-FUNGIBLE COLLATERAL IN ITS POSSESSION IDENTIFIABLE, AND 3) MUST APPLY MONEY OR FUNDS RECEIVED FROM COLLATERAL IN ITS POSSESSION OR CONTROL TO REDUCE SECURED OBLIGATION OR REMIT TO DEBTOR	1) MAY USE OR OPERATE COLLATERAL IN ITS POSSESSION: • FOR PURPOSE OF PRESERVING COLLATERAL OR ITS VALUE, • AS PERMITTED BY COURT ORDER, OR • EXCEPT FOR CONSUMER GOODS, AS AGREED BY DEBTOR 2) MAY HOLD AS ADDITIONAL SECURITY ANY NON-MONEY PROCEEDS, AND 3) MAY CREATE SECURITY INTEREST IN COLLATERAL	1) REASONABLE EXPENSES INCURRED IN CUSTODY, PRESERVATION, USE OR OPERATION OF COLLATERAL, AND 2) RISK OF ACCIDENTAL LOSS OR DAMAGE TO COLLATERAL IN EXCESS OF INSURANCE COVERAGE

The second group of duties imposed on a secured creditor relate to its obligations when a secured transaction is over. A secured transaction ends when there is no outstanding secured obligation and there is no commitment on the part of the secured party to provide additional value to the obligor. At that time, the secured party has certain duties aimed at undoing actions taken to perfect its security interest or collect on its collateral.

One of the sections imposing these duties was discussed in Chapter 4 in connection with perfection by filing. Under § 9-513, if a secured transaction has terminated, the secured party has an obligation to cause the secured party of record to file a termination statement within 20 days after the secured party receives an authenticated demand from the debtor or, if the collateral is consumer goods, within one month after the end of the transaction, whichever is earlier.

If the secured party perfected its security interest by taking control of a deposit account, electronic chattel paper, investment property, a letter-of-credit right or an electronic document, § 9-208 requires the secured party to take action to relinquish that control after the secured transaction ends within 10 days after receiving an authenticated demand by the debtor.

For secured creditors who sent a notification of assignment to account debtors pursuant to § 9-406(a) (discussed in Chapter 10), § 9-209 requires that they send an authenticated record releasing those account debtors from any further obligation to the secured party within 10 days after receiving an authenticated demand by the debtor after the secured transaction ends.

There is no special section in Article 9 dealing with the obligation of a secured party having possession of collateral to relinquish physical possession of the collateral when the secured transaction ends, but the tort law of conversion would provide a remedy to an aggrieved debtor if the secured party failed to do so.

A visualization of this duty to depart at the conclusion of a secured transaction follows:

DUTY OF SECURED PARTY WITH RESPECT TO COLLATERAL AT CONCLUSION OF SECURED TRANSACTION		
PERFECTION BY FILING	PERFECTION BY CONTROL	NOTIFICATION OF ACCOUNT DEBTORS
SECURED PARTY MUST CAUSE TERMINATION STATEMENT TO BE FILED WITHIN 20 DAYS AFTER DEMAND BY DEBTOR OR, IN CASE OF CONSUMER GOODS, WITHIN ONE MONTH AFTER END OF TRANSACTION § 9-513	SECURED PARTY MUST RELINQUISH CONTROL OVER DEPOSIT ACCOUNTS, ELECTRONIC CHATTEL PAPER, INVESTMENT PROPERTY, LETTER-OF-CREDIT RIGHT OR ELECTRONIC DOCUMENT WITHIN 10 DAYS AFTER DEMAND BY DEBTOR § 9-208	SECURED PARTY MUST RELEASE ACCOUNT DEBTORS PREVIOUSLY NOTIFIED OF ASSIGNMENT FROM FURTHER OBLIGATION TO SECURED PARTY WITHIN 10 DAYS AFTER DEMAND BY DEBTOR § 9-209

The final duty imposed on a secured party is a duty to respond to requests from a debtor for an accounting, a list of collateral or a statement of account. These requests are described in § 9-210, and allow a debtor to determine from the secured party what secured obligations are owing and what collateral secures those obligations. The secured party (other than a buyer of accounts, chattel paper, payments intangibles, or promissory notes or a consignor) must respond to any of these requests within 14 days after receipt. The secured party may not charge for its first response to a request in any six-month period, but may charge up to $25 for each additional response.

A visualization of the duty to respond to requests follows:

		DUTY OF SECURED PARTY TO RESPOND TO REQUESTS § 9-210		
		TYPES OF REQUESTS	TYPES OF RESPONSES	TIMING
REQUEST FOR ACCOUNTING		REQUESTS THAT SECURED PARTY PROVIDE ACCOUNTING OF UNPAID SECURED OBLIGATIONS FOR IDENTIFIED TRANSACTION	SEND AUTHENTICATED ACCOUNTING, OR DISCLAIM ANY INTEREST AND PROVIDE NAME AND ADDRESS OF SUCCESSOR SECURED PARTY	WITHIN 14 DAYS AFTER RECEIPT
REQUEST REGARDING LIST OF COLLATERAL		REQUESTS THAT SECURED PARTY APPROVE OR CORRECT LIST OF COLLATERAL FOR IDENTIFIED SECURED OBLIGATIONS	SEND AUTHENTICATED APPROVAL OR CORRECTION OR DISCLAIM ANY INTEREST IN COLLATERAL AND PROVIDE NAME AND ADDRESS OF SUCCESSOR SECURED PARTY	WITHIN 14 DAYS AFTER RECEIPT
REQUEST REGARDING STATEMENT OF ACCOUNT		REQUESTS THAT SECURED PARTY APPROVE OR CORRECT STATEMENT INDICATING AGGREGATE UNPAID SECURED OBLIGATION FOR IDENTIFIED TRANSACTION	SEND AUTHENTICATED APPROVAL OR CORRECTION OR DISCLAIM ANY INTEREST IN OBLIGATIONS AND PROVIDE NAME AND ADDRESS OF SUCCESSOR SECURED PARTY	WITHIN 14 DAYS AFTER RECEIPT

Chapter 10
RIGHTS OF THIRD PARTIES

Part 4 of Article 9 deals with the relationship between secured creditors and third parties, that is, persons other than the debtor. Most of its provisions relate to "account debtors" who are defined in § 9-102(a)(3) as persons obligated on accounts, chattel paper, or general intangibles (but not persons obligated to pay a negotiable instrument). When the account, chattel paper or general intangible on which such a third party is obligated becomes collateral, the third party is suddenly involved in a secured transaction it may know nothing about and wishes to ignore. Part 4 describes the extent to which this position may be foisted upon these third parties, and the rights and duties that flow from it.

The first issue addressed by Part 4 is whether the debtor may create a security interest in its rights in collateral if it is precluded from doing so by other law or contractual undertakings. The general rule, set forth in § 9-401(a), is that whether the debtor may transfer (voluntarily or involuntarily) rights in collateral is governed by law other than Article 9. There are, however, certain exceptions to this general rule.

The first exception appears in § 9-401(b). This provision deals with covenants between a debtor and a secured party precluding the debtor from transferring the debtor's rights in the collateral or making such a transfer a default (a so-called "negative pledge" clause). Such a clause might read as follows:

> Except as otherwise permitted by this agreement, the debtor shall not sell, assign (by operation of law or otherwise) or otherwise dispose of any of the collateral.

Section 9-401(b) provides that such a contractual provision does not prevent the transfer in violation of its terms from becoming effective. If the debtor violates such a provision, the secured party may exercise any remedies it has for breach. However, the transfer itself is not void or voidable, even if the negative pledge clause so states, and even if the transferee obtains priority to the collateral.

The second type of exception can be found in §§ 9-406(d), 9-407(a), 9-408(a) and 9-409(a). These provisions generally render ineffective contractual restrictions on security interests in certain types of collateral. Section 9-406 deals with security interests in accounts (other than "health-care-insurance receivables," § 9-102(a)(46)), chattel paper, payment intangibles, and promissory notes. Section 9-407 covers security interests in a lessee's interest under a lease contract or a lessor's residual interest in goods subject to a lease. Sales of promissory notes, sales of payment intangibles, security interests in health-care-insurance receivables and security interests in general intangibles that are not payment intangibles are covered by § 9-408. Section 9-409 deals with collateral consisting of letter-of-credit rights. All of these sections state that a contractual provision is "ineffective" to the extent that it "prohibits, restricts, or requires . . . consent" to creation, attachment, or perfection of a security interest in the collateral or provides that those actions give rise to a default or remedy. Sections 9-406 and 9-407 also render ineffective limitations on enforcement of a security interest in the collateral covered thereby.

Legal restrictions (as opposed to contractual restrictions) on the creation or enforcement of security interests are addressed in a third set of exceptions, in §§ 9-406(f) (for accounts (other than health-care-insurance receivables) and chattel paper), 9-408(c) (for promissory notes, payment intangibles, health-care-insurance receivables and general intangibles that are not payment intangibles) and 9-409(a) (for letter-of-credit rights). Again, these provisions generally render a "rule of law, statute, or regulation that prohibits, restricts, or requires the consent of a government, governmental body or official" ineffective insofar as they impair the creation, attachment or perfection of a security interest or create a default or remedy as a result. Unlike §§ 9-408 and 9-409, § 9-406 also covers legal restrictions on enforcement of security interests.

Sections 9-408 and 9-409 explicitly limit the scope of the provisions invalidating anti-assignment provisions of law or contract by stating that the security interest in a promissory note, health-care-insurance receivable, general intangible or letter-of-credit right conveyed in violation of otherwise valid provisions is not enforceable against the person obligated on the collateral unless that person agrees. Therefore, although a secured creditor may ascribe some value to the collateral in extending credit (perhaps assuming that an agreement with the obligor will be reached in the event of a default or that the collateral will generate proceeds to which its security interest will attach), the obligor will not be negatively affected in any way by the security interest. These protections are not given in § 9-406 to account debtors with respect to accounts or chattel paper.

A visualization of the provisions relating to transfer of a debtor's rights in collateral follows:

TRANSFER OF RIGHTS IN COLLATERAL

RULE	EXCEPTIONS			PROTECTION FOR OBLIGOR
	NEGATIVE PLEDGE	CONTRACTUAL RESTRICTIONS	LEGAL RESTRICTIONS	
WHETHER DEBTOR'S RIGHTS IN COLLATERAL MAY BE TRANSFERRED IS GOVERNED BY NON-ART. 9 LAW § 9-401(a)	AGREEMENT BETWEEN DEBTOR AND SECURED PARTY PROHIBITING TRANSFER OF DEBTOR'S RIGHTS IN COLLATERAL OR TRIGGERING DEFAULT DOES NOT MAKE TRANSFER INEFFECTIVE § 9-401(b)	CONTRACTUAL TERM IS INEFFECTIVE THAT PROHIBITS, RESTRICTS OR REQUIRES CONSENT TO ASSIGNMENT OR TRANSFER, OR CREATION, ATTACHMENT OR PERFECTION (OR FOR (1) AND (2) BELOW, ENFORCEMENT) OF SECURITY INTEREST OR TRIGGERING DEFAULT, FOR: 1) ACCOUNTS, CHATTEL PAPER, PAYMENT INTANGIBLES, PROMISSORY NOTES § 9-406(a) 2) LEASEHOLD INTERESTS OR RESIDUAL INTEREST OF LESSOR § 9-407(a) 3) SALE OF PROMISSORY NOTES, SALE OF PAYMENT INTANGIBLES, HEALTH-CARE-INSURANCE RECEIVABLES, GENERAL INTANGIBLES § 9-408(a) 4) LETTER-OF-CREDIT RIGHTS § 9-409(a)	RULE OF LAW, STATUTE OR REGULATION IS INEFFECTIVE THAT PROHIBITS, RESTRICTS OR REQUIRES CONSENT TO ASSIGNMENT OR TRANSFER, OR CREATION, ATTACHMENT OR PERFECTION (OR FOR (1) BELOW, ENFORCEMENT) OF SECURITY INTEREST OR TRIGGERING DEFAULT, FOR: 1) ACCOUNTS OR CHATTEL PAPER § 9-406(f) 2) PROMISSORY NOTES, HEALTH-CARE-INSURANCE RECEIVABLES, GENERAL INTANGIBLES § 9-408(c) 3) LETTER-OF-CREDIT RIGHTS § 9-409(a)	SECURITY INTEREST CREATED IN VIOLATION OF OTHERWISE VALID CONTRACTUAL OR LEGAL PROVISIONS RENDERED INEFFECTIVE BY ART. 9 IS NOT ENFORCEABLE AGAINST OBLIGOR ON PROMISSORY NOTES, HEALTH-CARE-INSURANCE RECEIVABLES, GENERAL INTANGIBLES OR LETTER-OF-CREDIT RIGHTS § 9-408(d) § 9-409(b)

A second issue addressed in Part 4 of Article 9 is the rights of the account debtor to assert defenses against an assignee. As a general matter, an assignee (such as a secured party) is subject to all terms of the agreement between the account debtor and the assignor, and any defense or claim in recoupment arising from the transaction giving rise to the contract may be asserted against the assignee by the account debtor, as can any other defense or claim accruing before the account debtor receives notice of the assignment. § 9-404(a).

However, an account debtor may make an agreement with an assignee not to assert against the assignee defenses or claims that the account debtor has against the assignor (other than defenses that may be asserted against a holder in due course of a negotiable instrument). Such an agreement is enforceable if the assignee takes the assignment for value, in good faith, without notice of a claim and without notice of a defense or claim in recoupment of the type that may be asserted against a person enforcing a negotiable instrument under § 3-305(a). § 9-403(b).

A visualization of these provisions governing the assertion of defenses against assignees follows:

ASSERTION OF DEFENSES AGAINST ASSIGNEES	
RULE § 9-404(a)	EXCEPTION § 9-403(b)
RIGHTS OF ASSIGNEE ARE SUBJECT TO ALL TERMS OF AGREEMENT BETWEEN ASSIGNOR AND ACCOUNT DEBTOR AND 1) ANY DEFENSE OR CLAIM IN RECOUPMENT ARISING FROM TRANSACTION GIVING RISE TO CONTRACT, AND 2) ANY OTHER DEFENSE OR CLAIM AGAINST ASSIGNOR ACCRUING BEFORE ACCOUNT DEBTOR RECEIVES NOTICE OF ASSIGNMENT AUTHENTICATED BY ASSIGNOR OR ASSIGNEE	AGREEMENT BETWEEN ACCOUNT DEBTOR AND ASSIGNOR NOT TO ASSERT CLAIMS OR DEFENSES IS ENFORCEABLE BY ASSIGNEE TAKING ASSIGNMENT 1) FOR "VALUE," § 3-303(a), 2) IN GOOD FAITH, 3) WITHOUT NOTICE OF CLAIM TO PROPERTY ASSIGNED, AND 4) WITHOUT NOTICE OF A § 3-305(b) DEFENSE OR CLAIM IN RECOUPMENT

Similarly, the account debtor generally may continue to make payments to the assignor to satisfy its contractual obligations despite the fact that the account, chattel paper or payment intangible on which it owes payment has been assigned to a secured party. However, once the account debtor receives a notification, authenticated by the assignor or the assignee, that the amount has been assigned and that payment is to be made to the assignee, the account debtor (other than one owing payment on a health-care-insurance receivable) may discharge its obligation only by paying the assignee and not by paying the assignor. § 9-406(a). The conditions under which such a notification may be sent are set forth in § 9-607(a) and will be discussed in Chapter 11.

The notification must meet the requirements of § 9-406(b), and the account debtor is entitled to request reasonable proof that the assignment has been made. If the notification is deficient, or the assignee does not provide reasonable proof, the account debtor may continue to pay the assignor. § 9-406(c).

A visualization of the provisions dealing with payments by an account debtor follows:

PAYMENTS BY ACCOUNT DEBTORS			
RULE	EXCEPTION		
ACCOUNT DEBTOR MAY CONTINUE TO PAY ASSIGNOR OF ACCOUNT, CHATTEL PAPER OR PAYMENT INTANGIBLE	TIMING § 9-406(a)	INEFFECTIVE NOTIFICATION § 9-406(b)	PROOF OF ASSIGNMENT § 9-406(c)
	AFTER RECEIPT OF EFFECTIVE NOTIFICATION AUTHENTICATED BY ASSIGNOR OR ASSIGNEE, ACCOUNT DEBTOR MUST PAY ASSIGNEE RATHER THAN ASSIGNOR	1) DOES NOT REASONABLY IDENTIFY RIGHTS ASSIGNED, 2) VALID AGREEMENT BETWEEN ACCOUNT DEBTOR AND SELLER OF PAYMENT INTANGIBLE PROVIDES FOR PAYMENT ONLY TO ASSIGNOR, OR 3) AT OPTION OF ACCOUNT DEBTOR, NOTIFICATION ASKS FOR LESS THAN FULL INSTALLMENT OWED	ACCOUNT DEBTOR MAY REQUEST REASONABLE PROOF OF ASSIGNMENT, AND NEED NOT COMPLY WITH NOTIFICATION IF NO PROOF PROVIDED § 9-406(c)

A final issue addressed by Part 4 of Article 9 is the impact of the secured transaction on the autonomy generally vested in the account debtor and the assignor over their contractual relationship giving rise to the collateral. Under § 9-405, modifications of, or substitutions for, an assigned contract are generally effective against an assignee so long as the right to payment has not been fully earned, or the right to payment has been fully earned but the account debtor has not received authenticated notification of the assignment from the assignor or the assignee under § 9-406(a).

Three protections are afforded assignees in respect of such modifications or substitutions: (1) the modifications must be made in good faith; (2) the assignee gets corresponding rights under the modified or substituted contract; and (3) the assignment may make such a modification or substitution a breach of contract giving rise to a default.

A visualization of these provisions governing modification of or substitution for an assigned contract follows:

MODIFICATION OF OR SUBSTITUTION FOR ASSIGNED CONTRACT § 9-405	
WHEN EFFECTIVE	**PROTECTIONS FOR SECURED PARTY**
RIGHT TO PAYMENT NOT FULLY EARNED BY PERFORMANCE, OR RIGHT TO PAYMENT FULLY EARNED BY PERFORMANCE BUT ACCOUNT DEBTOR HAS NOT RECEIVED § 9-406(a) NOTIFICATION OF ASSIGNMENT	MUST BE MADE IN GOOD FAITH, ASSIGNEE ACQUIRES CORRESPONDING RIGHTS UNDER MODIFIED OR SUBSTITUTED CONTRACT, AND ASSIGNMENT MAY PROVIDE THAT MODIFICATION OR SUBSTITUTION IS BREACH OF CONTRACT

Chapter 11
DEFAULT AND REMEDIES

One of the major advantages of being a secured creditor is the ability to enforce a security interest in the collateral after a debtor's default consistent with the provisions of Article 9. Part 6 of Article 9 sets forth the rights and remedies of the secured creditor, and limitations on the actions the secured creditor may take. It also provides remedies to those harmed by improper creditor actions.

We will begin by looking at the various methods provided by Article 9 for enforcement of security interests upon default, and will then examine protections afforded those who are damaged by the failure of the secured creditor to follow the rules.

A. ENFORCEMENT OF SECURITY INTEREST

Article 9 provides five basic mechanisms for enforcing security interests. A visualization of these five options follows:

CREDITORS' REMEDIES
1) REDUCING CLAIM TO JUDGMENT § 9-601(a)(1)
2) COLLECTION AND ENFORCEMENT § 9-607
3) REPOSSESSION § 9-609
4) DISPOSITION § 9-610
5) STRICT FORECLOSURE § 9-620

We will discuss each of these options in turn.

1. Judicial Enforcement

The availability of remedies under Article 9 does not limit the ability of a secured creditor after default to pursue the same remedies an unsecured creditor may pursue to enforce a debt. Under § 9-601(a)(1), a secured creditor may reduce its claim to judgment, and enforce the claim by any available judicial procedure. Except to the extent precluded by non-Article 9 law, the rights to pursue judicial enforcement and those enforcement mechanisms provided under Article 9 are "cumulative and may be exercised simultaneously." § 9-601(c). Sale of collateral following execution on the collateral is deemed to be foreclosure of the security interest under Article 9, except that the sale is covered by non-Article 9 law, and the secured creditor may purchase at the sale. § 9-601(f). The lien of a levy on collateral through judicial means has priority against other creditors from the earliest of the date of perfection of the security interest and the date a financing statement was filed; the interest in the collateral does not date from the time of the levy. § 9-601(e).

A visualization of the provisions dealing with judicial enforcement follows:

	RIGHT TO PURSUE § 9-601(a)	RIGHTS CUMULATIVE § 9-601(c)	LEVY ON COLLATERAL § 9-601(e)	EXECUTION SALE § 9-601(f)
JUDICIAL ENFORCEMENT	AFTER DEFAULT, SECURED PARTY MAY REDUCE CLAIM TO JUDGMENT, FORECLOSE OR OTHERWISE ENFORCE BY AVAILABLE JUDICIAL PROCEDURE	RIGHTS UNDER ART. 9 AND RIGHT TO PURSUE JUDICIAL FORECLOSURE ARE CUMULATIVE AND MAY BE EXERCISED AT SAME TIME	LIEN CREATED BY LEVY UPON EXECUTION DATES TO EARLIEST OF: 1) DATE OF PERFECTION, OR 2) DATE OF FILING	EXECUTION SALE IS ART. 9 FORECLOSURE OF SECURITY INTEREST AND SECURED PARTY MAY PURCHASE AT SALE

2. Collection and Enforcement

If the collateral is the type on which a third party (not the debtor) is obligated, such as accounts, chattel paper, payment intangibles, promissory notes and deposit accounts, § 9-607(a) permits the secured party, if the parties have so agreed but in any event after a default, to take certain actions to enforce and collect from that collateral.

First, the secured party may notify the "account debtor," § 9-102(a)(3), or other person obligated on the collateral, to pay the secured party directly.

Second, the secured party may take any proceeds of the collateral to which it is entitled. Third, it may enforce the obligations of the account debtor or other person obligated on the collateral to make payment or render performance on the collateral, and may exercise the rights of the debtor with respect to any property securing those obligations. And fourth, if the collateral is a deposit account, it may either apply the balance in the deposit account to the secured obligation (if it is the bank with which the account is maintained) or may direct the bank to pay the balance to the secured party (if it is not the bank and has control over the account). The actions the secured party takes must in any event be commercially reasonable if it has recourse to the debtor or a secondary obligor for any deficiency. § 9-607(c).

A visualization of the secured party's right to collect and enforce third party obligations follows:

RIGHT TO COLLECT AND ENFORCE § 9-607	
RIGHTS OF CREDITOR	**DUTIES OF CREDITOR**
NOTIFY ACCOUNT DEBTORS AND OTHER OBLIGORS TO PAY SECURED PARTY DIRECTLY, TAKE PROCEEDS, ENFORCE THIRD PARTY OBLIGATIONS TO PAY OR PERFORM ON COLLATERAL AND ENFORCE RIGHTS OF DEBTOR WITH RESPECT TO PROPERTY SECURING THOSE OBLIGATIONS, AND TAKE DEPOSIT ACCOUNT COLLATERAL	COLLECT IN COMMERCIALLY REASONABLE MANNER UNLESS THERE IS NO RECOURSE TO DEBTOR OR SECONDARY OBLIGOR WITH RESPECT TO COLLATERAL

Any cash proceeds received by the secured party upon collection or enforcement of the collateral goes first to pay the reasonable expenses of collection and enforcement, second to satisfy the secured obligation, and third to satisfy any subordinate security interest if the secured party receives an authenticated demand from that subordinate secured party before distribution of the proceeds is complete. § 9-608(a)(1). If there are excess cash proceeds, they are paid to the debtor (and the obligor remains liable for any deficiency) unless the underlying transaction is a sale of accounts chattel paper, payment intangibles, or promissory notes. §§ 9-608(a)(4) and 9-608(b). Noncash proceeds need not be distributed unless failure to do so would be commercially unreasonable. § 9-608(a)(3).

A visualization of the provisions on application of proceeds of collection and enforcement of collateral follows:

APPLICATION OF PROCEEDS OF COLLECTION AND ENFORCEMENT
§ 9-608

CASH PROCEEDS	NON-CASH PROCEEDS
1) REASONABLE EXPENSES OF COLLECTION, ENFORCEMENT, TAKING, HOLDING, PREPARING FOR DISPOSITION, PROCESSING, DISPOSING OF COLLATERAL AND, IF PROVIDED BY AGREEMENT AND NOT PROHIBITED BY LAW, REASONABLE ATTORNEYS' FEES AND EXPENSES OF SECURED PARTY	NO OBLIGATION TO APPLY OR PAY OVER UNLESS FAILURE IS NOT COMMERCIALLY REASONABLE
2) SATISFACTION OF SECURED OBLIGATIONS	
3) SATISFACTION OF OBLIGATIONS SECURED BY SUBORDINATE SECURITY INTEREST IN COLLATERAL IF TIMELY REQUEST MADE	
IF NOT SALE OF ACCOUNTS, CHATTEL PAPER, PAYMENT INTANGIBLES OR PROMISSORY NOTES 4) SURPLUS TO DEBTOR AND OBLIGOR LIABLE FOR DEFICIENCY IF SALE OF ACCOUNTS, CHATTEL PAPER, PAYMENT INTANGIBLES OR PROMISSORY NOTES 4) NO SURPLUS TO DEBTOR AND OBLIGOR NOT LIABLE FOR DEFICIENCY	

3. Right to Take Possession

For tangible collateral, § 9-609(a) gives the secured party the right, after default, to take possession of the collateral or, in the case of equipment, to leave the equipment in the debtor's possession but render it unusable and dispose of it there. The latter option might be employed if the equipment is too cumbersome or expensive to remove. If the secured party does not employ judicial process in taking these actions, § 9-609(b)(2) provides that it may not breach the peace in pursuing its rights.

Even before a default, if the debtor has so agreed, and in any event after a default, the secured party may require the debtor to assemble the collateral and make it available to the secured party at a place designated by the secured party that is reasonably convenient to both parties. § 9-609(c).

A visualization of the provisions of § 9-609 on the right to take possession of collateral follows:

RIGHT TO TAKE POSSESSION OF COLLATERAL § 9-609	
RIGHTS OF SECURED PARTY	**LIMITATIONS ON SECURED PARTY**
TAKE POSSESSION OF COLLATERAL	ONLY AFTER DEFAULT IF NO JUDICIAL PROCESS, NO BREACH OF THE PEACE
RENDER EQUIPMENT UNUSABLE AND DISPOSE OF IT ON DEBTOR'S PREMISES	ONLY AFTER DEFAULT IF NO JUDICIAL PROCESS, NO BREACH OF THE PEACE
REQUIRE DEBTOR TO ASSEMBLE COLLATERAL AT CONVENIENT LOCATION DESIGNATED BY SECURED PARTY	AFTER DEFAULT OR IF SO AGREED

4. Disposition of Collateral

In most cases, the goal of a secured creditor after default is to turn the collateral into cash that can be applied to the debt of the obligor. One way of accomplishing this goal is to dispose of the collateral to someone for cash. Section 9-610 provides the secured party the right to do this, so long as every aspect of the disposition, including "the method, manner, time, place, and other terms," are "commercially reasonable."

The fact that a disposition of the collateral by a different method or at a different time could have achieved a greater amount is not "of itself sufficient" to preclude the secured party from establishing that its disposition was commercially reasonable. § 9-627(a). Three types of disposition always meet the statutory requirement: a disposition in the usual manner on any recognized market; a disposition at the price current in any recognized market at the time of disposition; and a disposition in conformity with reasonable commercial practices among dealers in the type of property being disposed of. § 9-627(b). Although not required, approval of the disposition by a court, bona fide creditors' committee, representative of creditors or assignee for the benefit of creditors also establishes commercial reasonableness. § 9-627(c).

A visualization of the provisions relating to "commercially reasonable" dispositions follows:

COMMERCIALLY REASONABLE DISPOSITIONS § 9-627		
DISPOSITION MAY BE COMMERCIALLY REASONABLE EVEN IF:	DISPOSITION IS COMMERCIALLY REASONABLE IF:	
GREATER AMOUNT COULD HAVE BEEN OBTAINED BY DISPOSITION AT DIFFERENT TIME OR IN DIFFERENT METHOD	MADE: 1) IN USUAL MANNER ON ANY RECOGNIZED MARKET, 2) AT PRICE CURRENT IN ANY RECOGNIZED MARKET AT TIME OF DISPOSITION, OR 3) IN CONFORMITY WITH REASONABLE COMMERCIAL PRACTICES AMONG DEALERS IN SAME TYPE OF PROPERTY	APPROVED: 1) IN JUDICIAL PROCEEDING, 2) BY BONA FIDE CREDITORS' COMMITTEE, 3) BY REPRESENTATIVE OF CREDITORS, OR 4) BY ASSIGNEE FOR BENEFIT OF CREDITORS (APPROVAL IS NOT REQUIRED)

Within the constraints of commercial reasonableness, the secured party is given significant flexibility in structuring its disposition. It may dispose of the collateral by sale, lease, license, or other type of disposition. § 9-610(a). It may use public proceedings (meaning "one at which the price is determined after the public has had a meaningful opportunity for competitive bidding," Official Comment 7 to § 9-610) or engage in a private disposition, § 9-610(b). The secured party may not purchase the collateral at a private disposition unless the collateral is "of a kind that is customarily sold on a recognized market or the subject of widely distributed standard price quotations," such as a stock exchange. § 9-610(c). It may dispose of the collateral by one or more contracts, as a unit or in parcels, and at any time and place and on any terms. § 9-610(b). Although a contract for disposition of the collateral generally includes warranties as to title usual for a contract for the voluntary disposition of property, § 9-610(d), the secured party may disclaim those warranties. § 9-610(e).

A visualization of the right to dispose of collateral under § 9-610 follows:

DISPOSITION OF COLLATERAL AFTER DEFAULT § 9-610	
RIGHTS OF SECURED PARTY	LIMITATIONS ON SECURED PARTY
MAY SELL, LEASE, LICENSE OR OTHERWISE DISPOSE OF COLLATERAL, PUBLIC OR PRIVATE PROCEEDINGS, ONE OR MORE CONTRACTS, AS UNIT OR IN PARCELS, AT ANY TIME AND PLACE, ON ANY TERMS, AND MAY DISCLAIM WARRANTIES	METHOD, MANNER, TIME, PLACE, AND OTHER TERMS OF DISPOSITION MUST BE COMMERCIALLY REASONABLE, AND SECURED PARTY MAY PURCHASE COLLATERAL AT PRIVATE DISPOSITION ONLY IF COLLATERAL IS OF A KIND CUSTOMARILY SOLD ON RECOGNIZED MARKET OR IS SUBJECT OF WIDELY DISTRIBUTED STANDARD PRICE QUOTES

In most cases, the secured party may not pursue its right to dispose of collateral until it has given a reasonable authenticated notification to the appropriate parties of its intention. § 9-611(b). Several sections of Part 6 of Article 9 bear on this notice. The issues addressed include those cases in which notice does *not* have to be given, to whom notice must be sent, when notice must be sent, how one "sends" notice, and what is in the notice that is sent.

Section 9-611(d) identifies those situations in which prior notification of a disposition of the collateral by the secured party is excused based on the nature of the collateral. There are three exceptions: perishable collateral, collateral that threatens to decline speedily in value, and collateral that is of a type customarily sold on a recognized market (such as a stock exchange).

The persons entitled to receive notice are specified in § 9-611(c). The "debtor," § 9-102(a)(28), is entitled to notice, as is any "secondary obligor," § 9-102(a)(71). These parties may waive their right to receive notice, but only by an agreement entered into and authenticated after default. § 9-624(a).

If the collateral is not "consumer goods," § 9-102(a)(23), certain other persons who may have an interest in the collateral must also be notified under § 9-611(c)(3). These include any person who has provided the secured party an authenticated notification of a claim to the collateral before the "notification date," § 9-611(a), any other secured party or lienholder with a security interest in or lien on the collateral perfected by a financing statement properly filed and of record ten days before the notification date, and any other secured party that held a security interest in the collateral ten days before the notification date perfected under a federal statute, regulation or treaty or pursuant to a certificate-of-title statute as described in § 9-311(a).

Section 9-311(e) provides a safe harbor for compliance with the obligation to notify competing UCC secured parties and lienholders. If the secured party requests, in a commercially reasonable manner, a UCC search for financing statements indexed under the debtor's name between 20 and 30 days before the notification date and either did not receive a response to the request or received a response and sent the notice to all those secured parties and lienholders listed on the response, the secured party is deemed to have met its burden to provide notice to competing UCC-perfected secured parties and lienholders, even if no notice was sent to them.

The timeliness of notice is addressed by § 9-612. Section 9-611(b) requires "reasonable" notice. Section 9-612(a) states that whether a notification is sent within a "reasonable" time is a "question of fact." However, in transactions other than "consumer transactions," § 9-102(a)(26), a post-default notification sent 10 days or more before the earliest time of disposition specified in the notification is deemed to be sent within a "reasonable time." § 9-612(b).

What does it mean to "send" a notification? The definition of "send" in § 9-102(a)(74) makes clear that a notification need not be received to be "sent." To "send" a notification the sender must do one of two things. First, the sender may deposit it in the mail, deliver it for transmission, or transmit it by any other usual means of communication, with postage or cost of transmission provided for, and addressed to any reasonable address. Alternatively, a notification is deemed to be "sent" if the sender causes it to be received by the recipient within the time it would have been received if properly mailed, delivered for transmission or transmitted.

The contents of the required notification are described in § 9-613 (for transactions other than a "consumer-goods transaction," § 9-102(a)(24)) and § 9-614 (for a "consumer-goods transaction"). In both cases, the notification must describe the debtor and the secured party, describe the collateral, state the method of intended disposition, state that the debtor is entitled to an accounting and any charges for that accounting, and state the time and place of a public disposition or the time after which any other disposition is to be made.

For a consumer-goods transaction, the notification must also include three additional pieces of information. It must describe any liability for a deficiency of the recipient of the notice, it must provide a telephone number from which the recipient may find out the amount necessary to redeem the collateral, and it must provide a telephone number or mailing address from which additional information is available.

Although no specific form is mandated, each of §§ 9-613 and 9-614 includes a form of notification that is sufficient to satisfy its requirements.

A visualization of notice issues relating to proposed dispositions of collateral follows:

NOTICE ISSUES

EXCEPTIONS § 9-611(d)	TO WHOM § 9-611(c)	WHEN § 9-612	HOW SENT § 9-102(a)(74)	CONTENTS §§ 9-613 & 9-614
PERISHABLE, THREATENS TO DECLINE SPEEDILY IN VALUE, OR CUSTOMARILY SOLD ON RECOGNIZED MARKET	DEBTOR § 9-102(a)(28) UNLESS POST-DEFAULT WAIVER § 9-624(a), SECONDARY OBLIGOR § 9-102(a)(71) UNLESS POST-DEFAULT WAIVER § 9-624(a), AND FOR NON-CONSUMER GOODS COLLATERAL, 1) OTHER PERSONS WHO GIVE NOTICE OF CLAIM, 2) OTHER SECURED PARTIES OR LIENHOLDERS IN UCC RECORDS 10 DAYS BEFORE NOTICE SENT, AND 3) OTHER SECURED PARTIES PERFECTED UNDER FEDERAL LAW OR CERTIFICATE-OF-TITLE STATUTE 10 DAYS BEFORE NOTICE SENT	NON-CONSUMER TRANSACTION: 10 DAYS PRIOR NOTICE IS REASONABLE CONSUMER TRANSACTION: QUESTION OF FACT	DEPOSIT IN MAIL, DELIVER FOR TRANSMISSION OR ANY OTHER USUAL MEANS OF COMMUNICATION WITH POSTAGE OR COST PROVIDED FOR ADDRESSED TO REASONABLE ADDRESS OR RECEIVED WITHIN SAME TIME AS IF SENT BY ONE OF USUAL MEANS	1) DEBTOR AND SECURED PARTY, 2) COLLATERAL, 3) METHOD OF DISPOSITION, 4) DEBTOR IS ENTITLED TO ACCOUNTING AND CHARGE THEREFOR, AND 5) TIME AND PLACE OF PUBLIC DISPOSITION OR TIME AFTER WHICH PRIVATE SALE IS TO BE MADE PLUS FOR CONSUMER-GOODS TRANSACTION: 6) LIABILITY FOR DEFICIENCY, 7) TELEPHONE NUMBER TO GET REDEMPTION AMOUNT, AND 8) TELEPHONE NUMBER OR MAILING ADDRESS FOR ADDITIONAL INFORMATION

A proper disposition of the collateral results in the receipt of proceeds by the secured party, and receipt of the collateral by the transferee. Section 9-615 provides direction on application of the proceeds. Noncash proceeds need not be applied or paid over for application unless the failure by the secured party to do so would be commercially unreasonable. § 9-615(c). Cash proceeds are applied, first, to pay the expenses of the disposition; second, to satisfy the secured obligation; third, to satisfy any subordinate security interest or lien for which a demand has been made; and fourth, to any consignor of the collateral from which a demand has been made. § 9-615(a). If there are excess proceeds, they are paid to the debtor unless the transaction was a sale of accounts, chattel paper, payment intangibles or promissory notes. If the proceeds are insufficient to satisfy the secured obligation in full, the obligor remains liable for any deficiency, unless the transaction was a sale of accounts, chattel paper, payment intangibles or promissory notes. § 9-615(d) and (e).

A visualization of the application of proceeds from a disposition of collateral follows:

APPLICATION OF PROCEEDS OF DISPOSITION OF COLLATERAL § 9-615	
CASH PROCEEDS	NONCASH PROCEEDS
1) REASONABLE EXPENSES OF RETAKING, HOLDING, PREPARING FOR DISPOSITION, PROCESSING AND DISPOSING OF COLLATERAL AND, IF PROVIDED BY AGREEMENT AND NOT PROHIBITED BY LAW, REASONABLE ATTORNEYS' FEES AND EXPENSES OF SECURED PARTY	NEED NOT BE APPLIED OR PAID OVER FOR APPLICATION UNLESS FAILURE TO DO SO WOULD BE COMMERCIALLY UNREASONABLE
2) SATISFACTION OF SECURED OBLIGATION	
3) SATISFACTION OF OBLIGATIONS SECURED BY SUBORDINATE SECURITY INTEREST OR LIEN, IF TIMELY DEMAND MADE	
4) CONSIGNOR, IF TIMELY DEMAND MADE	
IF NOT A SALE OF ACCOUNTS, CHATTEL PAPER, PAYMENT INTANGIBLES OR PROMISSORY NOTE	IF SALE OF ACCOUNTS, CHATTEL PAPER, PAYMENT INTANGIBLES OR PROMISSORY NOTE
5) SURPLUS TO DEBTOR AND OBLIGOR LIABLE FOR DEFICIENCY	5) NO SURPLUS TO DEBTOR AND OBLIGOR NOT LIABLE FOR DEFICIENCY

A good-faith transferee of the collateral in a disposition by the secured party takes all the debtor's rights in the collateral free of the security interest under which the disposition was made and any subordinate security interest or lien, even if the disposition failed to comply with the requirements of Article 9. § 9-617. A visualization of the rights of the transferee of collateral follows:

RIGHTS OF TRANSFEREES OF COLLATERAL § 9-617	
GOOD-FAITH TRANSFEREE	NON-GOOD-FAITH TRANSFEREE
DISPOSITION: 1) TRANSFERS ALL DEBTOR'S RIGHTS IN COLLATERAL, 2) DISCHARGES SECURITY INTEREST UNDER WHICH DISPOSITION MADE, AND 3) DISCHARGES ALL SUBORDINATE SECURITY INTERESTS AND LIENS	TAKES COLLATERAL SUBJECT TO: 1) DEBTOR'S RIGHTS IN COLLATERAL, 2) SECURITY INTEREST UNDER WHICH DISPOSITION IS MADE, AND 3) ANY OTHER SECURITY INTEREST OR LIEN

Pursuant to § 9-619, the secured party may provide the transferee of the collateral a "transfer statement" (which may be recorded) evidencing its acquisition of the debtor's rights in the collateral.

5. Acceptance in Satisfaction of Obligation

In some cases the secured creditor wishes to acquire the debtor's interest in the collateral rather than disposing of it pursuant to § 9-610. This process, familiarly known as "strict foreclosure," is described in § 9-620.

There are some secured transactions for which strict foreclosure is not available. If the secured creditor has a "purchase-money security interest," § 9-103, in "consumer goods," § 9-102(a)(23), and 60 percent of the cash price of the collateral has been paid, or if the secured creditor has a non-PMSI in consumer goods and 60 percent of the principal amount of the secured obligation has been paid, the secured party who has taken possession of the consumer goods must dispose of the collateral pursuant to § 9-610 within 90 days (unless the debtor and all secondary obligors agree in an authenticated agreement after default to a longer period). § 9-620(e) and (f). A debtor may waive the requirement for mandatory disposition of the collateral only by entering into an authenticated agreement after default. § 9-624(b).

In addition, acceptance of the collateral in partial satisfaction of the secured obligation is not available in a "consumer transaction," § 9-102(a)(26), although the secured creditor may accept collateral in full satisfaction of the secured obligation. § 9-620(g).

If the secured party wishes to pursue strict foreclosure in those situations where it is permitted to do so, it must first send a "proposal," § 9-102(a)(66), in which it describes the terms on which it is willing to accept the collateral in full or partial satisfaction of the secured obligation, to the persons listed in § 9-621. There are three persons to whom such a proposal must always be sent: any person who has given the secured party notice of a claim to the collateral before the debtor consents, any other person with a security interest in or lien on the collateral perfected by the filing of a financing statement properly of record 10 days before the debtor consents, and any other secured party that, 10 days before the debtor consents, held a security interest in the collateral perfected under federal law or a certificate-of-title statute. If the proposal reflects the wish of the secured party to accept the collateral in partial satisfaction of the secured obligation, the proposal must also be sent to any "secondary obligor," § 9-102(a)(71), who might be liable for any remaining secured obligation. Unlike § 9-611, § 9-621 does not provide a safe harbor to the secured creditor who relies on a UCC search conducted between 20 and 30 days before the debtor consents. Therefore, if the required notices are not provided, even if the failure is due to filing office error, the injured parties have a right to seek redress under § 9-625 for the secured party's non-compliance.

The second requirement for effective acceptance of the collateral is consent by the debtor. § 9-620(a)(1). There are two different forms of acceptance. § 9-620(c). First, the debtor may consent by agreeing to the terms of the acceptance in a record authenticated after default (*i.e.*, an express consent). Such a consent is effective both in the case of an acceptance in full satisfaction of the secured obligation and an acceptance in partial satisfaction of the secured obligation. Second, in the case of an acceptance in full satisfaction of the secured obligation only, the debtor's consent may be implied (*i.e.*, a deemed consent). The debtor consents if the secured party sends to the debtor after default a proposal for acceptance of the collateral in full satisfaction of the secured obligation that is unconditional (or subject only to the condition that the collateral not in the secured party's possession be preserved or maintained), and the secured party does not receive an authenticated notice of objection from the debtor within 20 days after sending the proposal. In this case, silence equals consent.

The third requirement for effective acceptance of the collateral is that the secured party has not received a timely notification of objection from any of the persons to whom the proposal was sent, or from any other person, other than the debtor, holding a subordinate security interest in the collateral. § 9-620(a)(2). Such an objection is timely if it is received by the secured party within 20 days after notification was sent to the person objecting or, if the person was not notified, within 20 days after the last notification was sent out (or if no notifications were sent, before the debtor consents to the acceptance). § 9-620(d).

The final requirement for effective acceptance of the collateral is that, if the collateral is consumer goods, the collateral is not in the possession of the debtor when the debtor consents to the acceptance.

There is no such thing as a "deemed" strict foreclosure; acceptance of the collateral in full or partial satisfaction of the secured obligation takes place only if the four requirements set forth above are satisfied, and if the secured creditor consents to the acceptance in an authenticated record or sends a proposal to the debtor. § 9-620(b).

A visualization of the requirements for acceptance of collateral in full or partial satisfaction of the secured obligation follows:

REQUIREMENTS FOR ACCEPTANCE OF COLLATERAL IN SATISFACTION OF SECURED OBLIGATION § 9-620

ACCEPTANCE PERMITTED	PROPOSAL SENT § 9-621	DEBTOR CONSENTS	NO TIMELY OBJECTION	CONSUMER GOODS
NO ACCEPTANCE IN PARTIAL SATISFACTION OF SECURED OBLIGATION IN CONSUMER TRANSACTION § 9-620(g) SECURED PARTY MUST CONDUCT § 9-610 DISPOSITION OF CONSUMER GOODS WITHIN 90 DAYS IF: 1) PMSI – 60% CASH PRICE PAID 2) NON-PSMI – 60% PRINCIPAL AMOUNT OF SECURED OBLIGATION PAID § 9-620(e)	1) PERSONS GIVING NOTICE OF CLAIM BEFORE DEBTOR CONSENTS, 2) SECURED PARTIES AND LIENHOLDERS IN UCC RECORDS 10 DAYS BEFORE DEBTOR CONSENTS, 3) OTHER SECURED PARTIES PERFECTED UNDER FEDERAL LAW OR CERTIFICATE-OF-TITLE STATUTE 10 DAYS BEFORE DEBTOR CONSENTS, AND 4) IF PARTIAL SATISFACTION, ANY SECONDARY OBLIGOR	EXPRESS CONSENT FOR ACCEPTANCE IN FULL OR PARTIAL SATISFACTION OF DEBT = DEBTOR PROVIDES AUTHENTICATED RECORD AFTER DEFAULT	DEEMED CONSENT FOR ACCEPTANCE IN FULL SATISFACTION OF DEBT = 1) SECURED PARTY SENDS PROPOSAL TO DEBTOR AFTER DEFAULT, 2) SECURED PARTY PROPOSES TO ACCEPT COLLATERAL IN SATISFACTION OF DEBT, AND 3) NO OBJECTION WITHIN 20 DAYS AFTER PROPOSAL SENT	FROM PERSON ENTITLED TO NOTICE OF PROPOSAL WITHIN 20 DAYS AFTER PROPOSAL SENT, OR FROM ANY OTHER PERSON OTHER THAN DEBTOR HOLDING SUBORDINATE INTEREST IN COLLATERAL WITHIN 20 DAYS AFTER LAST PROPOSAL SENT (OR IF NO PROPOSALS SENT, BEFORE DEBTOR CONSENTS)	CONSUMER GOODS COLLATERAL IS NOT IN POSSESSION OF DEBTOR

If the secured party accepts collateral in full or partial satisfaction of the secured obligation, the consequences described in § 9-622 are similar to those of a disposition of collateral pursuant to § 9-617. The secured party acquires all of the debtor's rights in the collateral, the secured obligation is discharged to the extent consented to by the debtor, the security interest and any subordinate encumbrances are discharged and any subordinate interest in the collateral is terminated. A visualization of § 9-622 follows:

CONSEQUENCES OF STRICT FORECLOSURE § 9-622
1) SECURED OBLIGATION DISCHARGED TO EXTENT DEBTOR CONSENTED,
2) TRANSFER TO SECURED PARTY OF DEBTOR'S RIGHTS IN COLLATERAL,
3) SECURITY INTEREST DISCHARGED AND ANY SUBORDINATE SECURITY INTEREST OR LIEN DISCHARGED, AND
4) OTHER SUBORDINATE INTERESTS IN COLLATERAL TERMINATED

B. RIGHTS AND REMEDIES OF DEBTOR AND THIRD PARTIES

Article 9 provides debtors and other parties protections in connection with the secured creditor's exercise of its remedies. The secured creditor may also be liable for damages caused by its noncompliance with its obligations under Article 9, or may have its ability to collect any deficiency impaired.

1. Redemption

A debtor, any "secondary obligor," § 9-102(a)(71), or any other secured party has the right to redeem collateral from a secured party exercising its remedies. § 9-623(a). Redemption must occur before the applicable remedy (collection, disposition or acceptance of collateral) is completed. In order to redeem collateral, the person seeking redemption must tender fulfillment of all secured obligations (meaning payment in full of all monetary obligations then due and performance in full of all non-monetary obligations then matured), plus reasonable expenses and attorneys' fees to the extent they would be paid upon disposition of the collateral under § 9-615(a)(1).

A debtor or secondary obligor may waive the right to redeem collateral by entering into an authenticated agreement after default. § 9-624(c). However, no such waiver is effective in a "consumer-goods transaction," § 9-102(a)(24).

A visualization of the provisions relating to the right of redemption follows:

RIGHT OF REDEMPTION
§ 9-623

WHO	WHEN	REQUIREMENTS	WAIVER
1) DEBTOR, 2) SECONDARY OBLIGOR, OR 3) OTHER SECURED PARTY OR LIENHOLDER	BEFORE SECURED PARTY HAS 1) COLLECTED COLLATERAL UNDER § 9-607, 2) DISPOSED OF COLLATERAL OR ENTERED CONTRACT FOR DISPOSITION UNDER § 9-610, OR 3) ACCEPTED COLLATERAL IN FULL OR PARTIAL SATISFACTION OF THE SECURED OBLIGATION UNDER § 9-622	PARTY REDEEMING TENDERS 1) FULFILLMENT OF ALL SECURED OBLIGATIONS, AND 2) REASONABLE EXPENSES AND, IF PROVIDED IN AGREEMENT AND PERMITTED BY LAW, REASONABLE ATTORNEYS' FEES AND LEGAL EXPENSES DESCRIBED IN § 9-615(a)(1)	DEBTOR OR SECONDARY OBLIGOR MAY WAIVE BY POST-DEFAULT AGREEMENT EXCEPT IN CONSUMER-GOODS TRANSACTION § 9-624(c)

2. Remedies for Non-compliance

If the secured party fails to satisfy its obligations under Article 9, § 9-625 provides four different remedies, depending on the nature of the secured party's non-compliance. First, the court may provide injunctive relief in the form of an order mandating or precluding action with respect to the collateral. Second, the court may award to the debtor, an obligor, or any person with a security interest in or other lien on the collateral compensatory damages for any loss caused by failure to comply. Third, for certain types of violations of Article 9, the court may award statutory damages to a debtor or "consumer obligor," § 9-102(a)(25). These include the failure to comply with certain enumerated provisions, as well as breach of any obligation (other than one imposed by § 9-616, *see* § 9-628(d)) if the goods are consumer goods. Finally, if the secured party fails to provide a list of collateral or a statement of account when requested to do so under § 9-210 (discussed in Chapter 9), the secured party may be bound by a list or statement included in the request as against a person who is reasonably misled by the failure.

A visualization of the remedies for the secured party's non-compliance with the requirements of Article 9 follows:

REMEDIES FOR NON-COMPLIANCE § 9-625			
INJUNCTIVE	COMPENSATORY DAMAGES	STATUTORY DAMAGES	LIMITATION OF SECURITY INTEREST
REQUIRE OR ENJOIN COLLECTION, ENFORCEMENT OR DISPOSITION OF COLLATERAL ON APPROPRIATE TERMS AND CONDITIONS	DAMAGES FOR ANY LOSS CAUSED BY FAILURE TO COMPLY, INCLUDING THOSE RELATING TO ALTERNATIVE FINANCING	$500 FOR VIOLATION OF §§ 9-208, 9-209, 9-509(a), 9-513(a) OR (c), OR 9-616(b)(2) OR PATTERN OF NON-COMPLIANCE WITH § 9-616(b)(1) OR FAILURE TO COMPLY WITHOUT REASONABLE CAUSE WITH § 9-210 REQUEST FOR CONSUMER GOODS COLLATERAL, CREDIT SERVICE CHARGE PLUS 10% OF PRINCIPAL AMOUNT OF OBLIGATION OR TIME-PRICE DIFFERENTIAL PLUS 10% OF CASH PRICE	FOR FAILURE TO COMPLY WITH § 9-210 REQUEST REGARDING LIST OF COLLATERAL OR STATEMENT OF ACCOUNT, SECURITY INTEREST MAY BE LIMITED AS SHOWN ON STATEMENT ACCOMPANYING REQUEST

The secured party has no duties as an Article 9 secured party to a person who is a debtor or obligor unless the person is known by the secured party to be a debtor or obligor, whose identity is known to the secured party, and the secured party knows how to communicate with that person. § 9-605. Moreover, the secured party has no liability to an unknown debtor or obligor, nor to a secured party or lienholder that has filed a financing statement against such a person, for failure to comply with Article 9 or by reason of its status as an Article 9 secured party. § 9-628.

Because Article 9 imposes special requirements on secured parties in consumer transactions and consumer-goods transactions, *see, e.g.*, §§ 9-614, 9-616 and 9-620, the secured party is protected from liability in the event it held a "reasonable belief" that the transaction was not a consumer-goods transaction or a consumer transaction or that the goods were not consumer goods based on a representation by the debtor or obligor with respect to use of the collateral or the purpose of the secured obligation. § 9-628(c).

The remedies provided by § 9-625 do not preempt other state law remedies that may be available to a person harmed by the wrongful conduct of a secured party. These include not only remedies for breach of contract, but also remedies for tort (such as assault, conversion, battery, trespass, and breach of the peace). Tort remedies may include punitive damages in appropriate cases.

3. Remedies Relating to Deficiency

Generally speaking, when a secured party collects or enforces collateral under § 9-607 or disposes of collateral under § 9-610 (other than in connection with a sale of accounts, chattel paper, payments intangibles, or promissory notes) for less than the full amount of the secured obligation, or accepts collateral in partial satisfaction of the secured obligation under § 9-620, the obligor remains liable for any remaining portion of the secured obligation. §§ 9-608(a)(4), 9-615(d) and 9-622(a)(1). In such a case, the secured party may follow its realization upon the collateral with an action against the obligor in personam seeking the deficiency.

In such an action, the obligor may seek to relieve itself of its obligation for the deficiency by asserting that the secured party violated its obligations under Article 9 with respect to the collateral. If the transaction was not a "consumer transaction," § 9-102(a)(26), the secured party is subject to the special rules in § 9-626 in any actions in which the deficiency (or any surplus collected by the secured party in excess of the secured obligation) is at issue.

Section 9-626 first allocates the burden of proof in such an action. The secured party need not establish its compliance with Article 9 unless the debtor or secondary obligor places the secured party's compliance in issue. Once that occurs, the secured party has the burden of establishing that it met its obligations under Article 9.

If the secured party fails to meet its burden of proof, the deficiency is computed according to the "rebuttable presumption rule." Section 9-626(a)(4) creates a presumption that, if the secured party had complied with its Article 9 obligations, the collateral would have been collected or enforced or sold for an amount sufficient to pay the secured obligation in full. The secured party is allowed to rebut this presumption by showing that a lesser amount would have been obtained even if the secured party had met its obligations. The deficiency is then computed based either on the presumption (which results in a deficiency of zero) or the lesser amount established by the secured party in rebuttal. As described in Official Comment 3 to § 9-626, "[u]nder this rebuttable presumption rule, the debtor or obligor is to be credited with the greater of the actual proceeds of the disposition or the proceeds that would have been realized had the secured party complied with the relevant provisions."

Section 9-626 does not operate in consumer transactions, and the drafters intended to leave to the court the determination of the proper rules in deficiency actions involving consumer transactions. Some courts may choose to apply the rebuttable presumption rule in those transactions as well. Others have applied the offset rule (which simply sets off any damage claim by the obligor against the deficiency sought by the secured party) or the "absolute bar rule" (which precludes any secured party which violates the requirements of Article 9 from seeking any deficiency). *See* Official Comment 4 to § 9-626.

Even if the secured party complies with its obligations under Article 9, if the disposition of collateral was to the secured party itself, or to a "person related to" the secured party, § 9-102(a)(62) and (63), or a secondary obligor, § 9-102(a)(71), and the amount of proceeds obtained was "significantly below the range of proceeds that a complying disposition" to another transferee would have brought, the deficiency (or surplus) is computed on the basis of the hypothetical amount a complying disposition to another person would have brought. § 9-615(f). In these cases of an alleged "low-price disposition," *see* Official Comment 6 to § 9-615, the debtor or obligor has the burden of establishing that the amount of proceeds is "significantly below the range of prices that a complying disposition" to another transferee would have brought.

These special rules relating to deficiency actions are visualized as follows:

B. RIGHTS AND REMEDIES OF DEBTOR AND THIRD PARTIES

REMEDIES RELATING TO DEFICIENCY

VIOLATION OF PART 6 § 9-626		LOW-PRICE SALE § 9-615(f)	
NON-CONSUMER TRANSACTION	CONSUMER TRANSACTION	CHARACTERISTICS	RESULT
1) BURDEN ON SECURED PARTY TO SHOW COMPLIANCE 2) IF SECURED PARTY FAILS, DEFICIENCY COMPUTED BASED ON HYPOTHETICAL AMOUNT OF PROCEEDS THAT WOULD HAVE RESULTED IF SECURED PARTY COMPLIED 3) HYPOTHETICAL AMOUNT PRESUMED TO BE AMOUNT OF SECURED OBLIGATION (REBUTTABLE PRESUMPTION RULE)	LEFT TO COURTS: 1) REBUTTABLE PRESUMPTION RULE, 2) OFFSET RULE, OR 3) ABSOLUTE BAR RULE	TRANSFEREE IS SECURED PARTY, "PERSON RELATED TO" SECURED PARTY, § 9-102(a)(62) & (63), OR "SECONDARY OBLIGOR," § 9-102(a)(71), AND DEBTOR OR OBLIGOR PROVES, § 9-626(a)(5), PROCEEDS SIGNIFICANTLY BELOW RANGE OBTAINABLE FROM OTHER TRANSFEREE	DEFICIENCY CALCULATED BASED ON AMOUNT OBTAINABLE FROM OTHER TRANSFEREE

Chapter 12
TRANSITION RULES

Article 9 was intended to take effect at a uniform time, July 1, 2001, upon enactment by each of the 50 states during the period after its promulgation by the American Law Institute and National Conference of Commissioners on Uniform State Laws in 1999. § 9-701. All states enacted by the specified effective date, although four states enacted non-uniform effective dates. Revised Article 9 became effective in Connecticut on October 1, 2001, and in Alabama, Mississippi and Florida on January 1, 2002.

Once the revisions became effective in a state, all transactions or liens within the scope of revised Article 9 became subject to its provisions, even if the transaction or lien was entered into or created prior to the effective date. § 9-702(a). However, because the revisions expanded the scope of Article 9 to cover transactions previously governed by other law, § 9-702(b) provides a savings clause providing that those pre-effective date transactions are not invalidated by the new revisions, and may continue to be governed by non-Article 9 law. Examples of these transactions include the creation of "agricultural liens," § 9-102(a)(5), or security interests in "commercial tort claims," § 9-102(a)(13), both of which are newly within the scope of Article 9, § 9-109(a)(2) and (d)(12).

Even in the case of transactions within the scope of Article 9 both before and after the revisions, the new law poses problems. Security interests may have attached prior to the effective date of the revisions, and may even be perfected under the old law, but the actions taken to achieve that status may or may not be sufficient under revised Article 9. Or the secured party may have taken action to perfect a security interest prior to the effective date of the revisions, but the security interest does not attach until after the effective date. Article 9 provides transition rules in Part 7 that provide guidance on pre-existing secured transactions that become subject to revised Article 9.

Assume the existence of a security interest created (that is, it has attached and become enforceable pursuant to § 9-203) before the revisions became effective. That security interest may have been perfected under the earlier version of Article 9, or not perfected. The first situation addressed by these transition rules is the security interest that was perfected under the old version of Article 9 as of the effective date of the revisions. Here there are two possibilities: the applicable requirements for perfection under old Article 9 also satisfy the perfection requirements under revised Article 9, or they do not.

Section 9-703(a) states that, if the pre-revision perfection requirements would also satisfy those of revised Article 9, no further action under revised Article 9 is necessary. On the other hand, if the requirements for enforceability or perfection were modified in the revisions such that the steps taken to achieve enforceability or perfection prior to the effective date would not suffice thereafter, § 9-703(b) provides that the security interest remains perfected for a period of one year after the effective date, but compliance with revised Article 9 is required to continue the effectiveness and perfection of the security interest after that one-year grace period.

The second situation addressed by the transition rules is the security interest that was enforceable before the revisions became effective, but that was not perfected under old Article 9 as of the effective date. Section 9-704 tells us that such a security interest remains enforceable for one year after the effective date and remains enforceable thereafter if the requirements of revised § 9-203 are satisfied (either before or after the effective date of the revisions). Such a security interest must be perfected, if it ever is, by compliance with revised Article 9, whether before or after the effective date. § 9-704(3). In other words, if the secured party took action to perfect its security interest prior to the effective date, and that action was insufficient under old Article 9 but would be sufficient under revised Article 9, the security interest would become perfected upon the effective date of the revisions.

A visualization of the transition rules relating to security interests that became effective prior to the effective date of the revisions to Article 9 follows:

IMPACT OF REVISED ARTICLE 9 ON SECURITY INTERESTS THAT ATTACHED PRIOR TO EFFECTIVE DATE

	PERFECTED SECURITY INTEREST		UNPERFECTED SECURITY INTEREST	
	ACTION TO PERFECT SUFFICIENT UNDER REVISED ART. 9	ACTION TO PERFECT NOT SUFFICIENT UNDER REVISED ART. 9	ENFORCEABILITY	PERFECTION
	NO FURTHER ACTION REQUIRED § 9-703(a)	REMAINS PERFECTED FOR ONE YEAR AFTER EFFECTIVE DATE REMAINS EFFECTIVE AND PERFECTED THEREAFTER ONLY UPON COMPLIANCE WITH REVISED ART. 9 § 9-703(b)	REMAINS ENFORCEABLE FOR ONE YEAR AFTER EFFECTIVE DATE REMAINS ENFORCEABLE THEREAFTER ONLY UPON COMPLIANCE WITH REVISED § 9-203 § 9-704(1) & (2)	BECOMES PERFECTED IF COMPLIANCE WITH REVISED ART. 9 § 9-704(3)

The transition rules also deal with the impact of the revisions on filings and other actions made or taken prior to the effective date that would have been sufficient to perfect a security interest under the old Article 9, but the security interest does not attach until after the effective date. As a result of § 9-702, the security interest will generally be governed by revised Article 9 if attachment occurs after the effective date. Under § 9-705(a), in the case of actions other than the filing of a financing statement, the pre-effective-date action remains effective to perfect a security interest that attaches up to one year after the effective date, but the security interest will become unperfected unless action to perfect it consistent with revised Article 9 is taken before the end of that one-year period.

A visualization of these rules follows:

IMPACT OF REVISED ARTICLE 9 ON PRE-EFFECTIVE DATE ACTIONS (OTHER THAN FILING) TAKEN TO PERFECT SECURITY INTERESTS THAT ATTACH AFTER EFFECTIVE DATE § 9-705(a)	
PERIOD OF PERFECTION	REPERFECTION REQUIREMENT
PRE-EFFECTIVE DATE ACTION IS EFFECTIVE TO PERFECT SECURITY INTEREST THAT ATTACHES WITHIN ONE YEAR AFTER EFFECTIVE DATE	ATTACHED SECURITY INTEREST BECOMES UNPERFECTED ONE YEAR AFTER EFFECTIVE DATE UNLESS PERFECTED UNDER REVISED ART. 9

If the action taken prior to the effective date was the filing of a financing statement, either that filing would satisfy the requirements of revised Article 9, or it would not. If it would, § 9-705(b) states that the filing is effective to perfect the security interest that attaches after the effective date. This is true even if the filing would not have been effective to perfect the security interest under old Article 9 because, for example, it was filed in a jurisdiction or location that would be appropriate under revised Article 9 but not under old Article 9. However, because the filing was not effective to perfect the security interest under old Article 9, perfection is deemed to occur only upon or after the effective date of the revisions (when the requirements of revised § 9-203 are also satisfied) and priority dates from that time. § 9-709. The effectiveness of such a filing may be extended by the filing of a continuation statement in the same location, § 9-705(d), as long as all requirements for a filing under revised Article 9 are met. The debtor need not authorize the filing of such a continuation statement. § 9-708.

A visualization of these rules relating to perfection of post-effective date security interests by pre-effective date filings that satisfy revised Article 9 follows:

IMPACT OF REVISED ART. 9 ON PRE-EFFECTIVE DATE FILINGS MADE IN COMPLIANCE WITH REVISED ART. 9 TO PERFECT SECURITY INTERESTS THAT ATTACH AFTER EFFECTIVE DATE

EFFECTIVENESS § 9-705(b)	PRIORITY § 9-709(b)	CONTINUATION § 9-705(d)	AUTHORIZATION § 9-708
PRE-EFFECTIVE DATE FILING COMPLYING WITH REVISED ART. 9 IS EFFECTIVE TO PERFECT POST-EFFECTIVE DATE SECURITY INTEREST	IF FILING DID NOT SATISFY OLD ART. 9, PRIORITY DATES FROM EFFECTIVE DATE	CONTINUATION STATEMENT MAY BE FILED IN SAME LOCATION AS ORIGINAL FILING IF ORIGINAL FILING WAS IN OFFICE PRESCRIBED BY REVISED ART. 9	SECURED PARTY OF RECORD MAY AUTHORIZE FILING OF CONTINUATION STATEMENT

If the action taken prior to the effective date was a filing which would have been appropriate under old Article 9 but would not satisfy the requirements of revised Article 9, § 9-705(c) nevertheless validates the filing, making it effective to perfect a security interest that attaches after the effective date, for a period up to the earlier of June 30, 2006 (familiarly called the "cut-off date") and the date the financing statement would have ceased to be effective under the law of the jurisdiction in which it was filed. However, the duration of the effectiveness of such a pre-revision financing statement cannot be extended by the filing of a continuation statement, § 9-705(d). Instead, the secured party must file an in lieu financing statement discussed below. The secured party of record may file such an in lieu financing statement without authorization by the debtor. § 9-708. Relative priorities established under old Article 9 are not affected by revised Article 9. § 9-709(a).

A visualization of these provisions dealing with pre-effective date filings that were sufficient to perfect a security interest under old Article 9 but do not comply with revised Article 9 as those filings relate to security interests that attach after the effective date follows:

IMPACT OF REVISED ART. 9 ON PRE-EFFECTIVE DATE FILINGS NOT IN COMPLIANCE WITH REVISED ART. 9 TO PERFECT SECURITY INTERESTS THAT ATTACH AFTER EFFECTIVE DATE			
EFFECTIVENESS § 9-705(c)	PRIORITY § 9-709(a)	CONTINUATION § 9-705(d), § 9-706	AUTHORIZATION § 9-708
FILING EFFECTIVE UNTIL EARLIER OF JUNE 30, 2006 OR DATE FILING EXPIRES UNDER LAW OF FILING JURISDICTION	IF RELATIVE PRIORITIES WERE ESTABLISHED UNDER OLD ART. 9, OLD ART. 9 DETERMINES PRIORITY	EFFECTIVENESS OF PRE-EFFECTIVE DATE FINANCING STATEMENT MAY NOT BE CONTINUED BY CONTINUATION STATEMENT EFFECTIVENESS OF PRE-EFFECTIVE DATE FINANCING STATEMENT MAY BE CONTINUED BY FILING IN LIEU FINANCING STATEMENT IN OFFICE REQUIRED BY REVISED ART. 9	SECURED PARTY OF RECORD MAY AUTHORIZE FILING OF IN LIEU STATEMENT

In order to continue the effectiveness of a pre-revision financing statement that does not satisfy the requirements of revised Article 9 beyond the cut-off date (or the date of its natural expiration under the law of the jurisdiction in which it was filed), the secured party may file an initial financing statement in the location specified by, and satisfying all requirements of, revised Article 9 before that time. § 9-706(a). This initial financing statement, commonly referred to as an "in lieu" financing statement, substitutes for a continuation statement for these pre-revision filings that do not comply with the new Article 9. Such an in lieu statement must not only satisfy the requirements of revised

Article 9, but must also identify the pre-effective-date financing statement to which it relates and indicate that the pre-effective-date financing statement remains effective. § 9-706(c). An in lieu financing statement continues the effectiveness of the pre-revision filing for the period provided in § 9-515 of revised Article 9 (or § 9-403 of old Article 9 if the in lieu financing statement was filed before the effective date). § 9-706(b).

A visualization of the requirements of an in lieu financing statement follows:

IN LIEU FINANCING STATEMENT § 9-706		
WHEN USED	REQUIREMENTS	EFFECT
PRE-EFFECTIVE-DATE FINANCING STATEMENT FILED IN OFFICE NOT APPROPRIATE UNDER REVISED ART. 9	1) SATISFIES PART 5 OF REVISED ART. 9, 2) IDENTIFIES PRE-EFFECTIVE-DATE FINANCING STATEMENT BY OFFICE, DATE OF FILING AND FILE NUMBERS, AND 3) INDICATES THAT PRE-EFFECTIVE-DATE FINANCING STATEMENT REMAINS EFFECTIVE	CONTINUES EFFECTIVENESS OF PRE-EFFECTIVE-DATE FINANCING STATEMENT FOR PERIOD PROVIDED IN: 1) § 9-515 IF FILED AFTER EFFECTIVE DATE, OR 2) § 9-403 OF OLD ART. 9 IF FILED BEFORE THE EFFECTIVE DATE

Amendments to pre-effective-date financing statements other than to continue their effectiveness are generally governed by revised Article 9. § 9-707(b). However, a pre-effective-date financing statement may be terminated by compliance with the law of the jurisdiction in which it was filed. § 9-707(b). Under § 9-707(e), such a financing statement may be terminated by filing in the office in which it was filed unless an in lieu financing statement has been filed in another office designated by revised Article 9.

Other amendments require that one of three conditions be satisfied. First, an amendment is effective if the pre-effective-date financing statement and the amendment are both filed in the office specified by revised Article 9. Alternatively, an amendment is effective if the amendment is filed in the office specified by revised Article 9 concurrently with, or after the filing in that office of, an in lieu financing statement. Third, an amendment is effective if the amended information is provided in an in lieu financing statement filed in the appropriate location under revised Article 9.

A visualization of the provisions relating to amendments to pre-effective-date financing statements follows:

AMENDMENTS TO PRE-EFFECTIVE-DATE FINANCING STATEMENTS § 9-707		
CONTINUATION	TERMINATION	OTHER AMENDMENTS
GOVERNED BY § 9-705(d) AND (f) AND § 9-706	GOVERNED BY REVISED ART. 9 OR LAW OF PLACE OF ORIGINAL FILING EFFECTIVE UPON FILING OF TERMINATION STATEMENT IN OFFICE WHERE ORIGINAL FILING MADE UNLESS IN LIEU FINANCING STATEMENT FILED ELSEWHERE	AMENDMENT EFFECTIVE IF: 1) PRE-EFFECTIVE DATE FINANCING STATEMENT AND AMENDMENT FILED IN OFFICE REQUIRED BY REVISED ART. 9, 2) AMENDMENT FILED IN OFFICE REQUIRED BY REVISED ART. 9 WITH OR AFTER IN LIEU FINANCING STATEMENT, OR 3) AMENDED INFORMATION IS PART OF IN LIEU FINANCING STATEMENT

TABLE OF STATUTES

[References are to pages.]

UNIFORM COMMERCIAL CODE (UCC)

Sec.	Page
1-201(b)(3)	26
1-201(b)(9)	78; 82
1-201(b)(12)	2
1-201(b)(16)	15; 16
1-201(b)(24)	22; 91
1-201(b)(25)	14; 15
1-201(b)(27)	14
1-201(b)(29)	41; 59
1-201(b)(30)	6; 41; 59; 62; 63; 69; 70; 71; 73; 90; 91; 105
1-201(b)(35)	2; 3; 105
1-201(b)(37)	26
1-203	2; 3; 4
1-203(a)	3
1-203(b)	3
1-203(c)	3
1-203(d)	3
1-204	25; 26
1-301(a)(1)	65
1-301(c)(1)	65
1-301(e)(1)	65
1-301(g)(8)	65
1-302(b)	151
2A-103(1)(u)	82; 83
2A-508(5)	32
2-326(1)	6
2-401	3; 32
2-505	32
2-711	32
3-104	19; 20
3-303(a)	158
3-305(a)	158
3-305(b)	158
4-210	32
5-102(a)(2)	21
5-102(a)(3)	21
5-102(a)(9)	21; 43
5-102(a)(10)	21; 43
5-102(a)(11)	43
5-114	10
5-114(c)	43
5-116	68
5-118	32
7-106	40; 44
7-201(b)	15; 16
8-102(a)(14)	21
8-102(a)(15)	21
8-102(a)(17)	21
8-106(a)	41
8-106(b)	41

UNIFORM COMMERCIAL CODE (UCC)—Cont.

Sec.	Page
8-106(c)	41
8-106(d)	41
8-106(e)	41
8-110(d)	67; 68
8-110(e)	67; 68
8-301	41; 42
8-301(a)	36; 37
8-501(a)	21
9-102	7; 18; 22
9-102(a)(1)	101; 102
9-102(a)(2)	2; 3; 12; 13; 32
9-102(a)(3)	155; 163
9-102(a)(5)	2; 5; 185
9-102(a)(6)	22; 63
9-102(a)(7)	26
9-102(a)(9)	144
9-102(a)(10)	67
9-102(a)(11)	2; 3; 13; 14
9-102(a)(12)	11
9-102(a)(13)	14; 15; 27; 185
9-102(a)(14)	21
9-102(a)(15)	21
9-102(a)(16)	21
9-102(a)(18)	62; 63
9-102(a)(19)	7
9-102(a)(20)	2; 7; 8
9-102(a)(21)	3
9-102(a)(23)	7; 8; 17; 19; 168; 173
9-102(a)(24)	33; 34; 169; 177
9-102(a)(25)	179
9-102(a)(26)	15; 27; 169; 173; 181
9-102(a)(27)	60
9-102(a)(28)	23; 24; 26; 54; 69; 168; 170
9-102(a)(29)	15; 103
9-102(a)(30)	15; 16
9-102(a)(31)	14
9-102(a)(32)	93
9-102(a)(33)	18; 19
9-102(a)(34)	5; 17; 19; 78
9-102(a)(35)	5; 17; 19; 78
9-102(a)(39)	47; 55
9-102(a)(40)	95
9-102(a)(41)	2; 3; 63; 93; 101
9-102(a)(42)	11; 12
9-102(a)(44)	16; 17; 78
9-102(a)(45)	9
9-102(a)(46)	12; 13; 32; 155
9-102(a)(47)	15; 19; 20
9-102(a)(48)	18; 19
9-102(a)(49)	20; 21; 40

[References are to pages.]

UNIFORM COMMERCIAL CODE (UCC)—Cont.

Sec.	Page
9-102(a)(51)	22
9-102(a)(52)	76
9-102(a)(53)	59; 99
9-102(a)(54)	59; 60; 99
9-102(a)(56)	28; 69; 142
9-102(a)(57)	90
9-102(a)(58)	144
9-102(a)(59)	23; 24
9-102(a)(60)	28
9-102(a)(61)	2; 11; 12
9-102(a)(62)	182; 183
9-102(a)(63)	182; 183
9-102(a)(64)	28; 142; 143
9-102(a)(65)	2; 3; 19
9-102(a)(66)	173
9-102(a)(67)	58; 60
9-102(a)(68)	87
9-102(a)(69)	13
9-102(a)(70)	50; 51; 65
9-102(a)(71)	168; 170; 174; 177; 182; 183
9-102(a)(72)	23; 24
9-102(a)(73)	25; 26
9-102(a)(74)	169; 170
9-102(a)(75)	11; 12
9-102(a)(77)	28
9-102(a)(78)	13; 14
9-102(a)(79)	55; 57
9-102(a)(80)	59; 60; 63
9-103	34; 97; 173
9-103(a)(1)	32
9-103(b)	32; 84
9-103(b)(1)	32; 33
9-103(c)	33
9-103(e)	33; 35
9-103(f)	34; 35
9-103(g)	34; 35
9-103(h)	34; 35
9-104	40; 42; 43
9-104(a)(3)	103; 104
9-105	40; 43; 44
9-106	36; 40; 41
9-106(b)	41
9-106(c)	41
9-107	40; 43
9-108	26; 27; 52
9-108(a)	26
9-109	1; 6; 9
9-109(1)	84
9-109(a)	1; 2; 4; 22
9-109(a)(1)	7; 92; 93
9-109(a)(2)	185
9-109(a)(3)	6; 11; 12; 14; 20
9-109(b)	9

UNIFORM COMMERCIAL CODE (UCC)—Cont.

Sec.	Page
9-109(c)	8; 10
9-109(d)	5; 9; 10
9-109(d)(2)	92
9-109(d)(4)–(7)	6
9-109(d)(10)	103
9-109(d)(12)	14; 185
9-109(d)(13)	15
9-201(a)	75; 125
9-203	28; 31; 185; 186; 188
9-203(a)	24
9-203(b)	24; 25; 27; 28
9-203(b)(3)	26; 27; 76; 77; 105; 123; 146; 147
9-203(d)	30; 54; 55; 69
9-203(d)(1)	28
9-203(d)(2)	29
9-203(e)	28; 30; 54
9-203(f)–(i)	27; 28
9-204	86
9-204(c)	86
9-206(c)	32
9-207	151; 152
9-207(a)	151
9-208	153; 180
9-209	153; 180
9-210	153; 154; 179; 180
9-301–9-307	65
9-301(1)	65; 68
9-301(2)	67; 68
9-301(3)	67
9-301(3)(A)	68
9-301(3)(B)	68
9-301(3)(C)	67; 68
9-301(4)	67; 68
9-302	65
9-303	68
9-303(b)	67
9-303(c)	67
9-304(b)	67
9-305	67
9-305(b)	67; 68
9-305(c)	67
9-306	68
9-307	65; 66; 68; 106
9-307(d)	66
9-307(g)	66
9-308	31
9-308(d)–(g)	47
9-309	32; 47; 87
9-309(1)	81
9-310	47; 58
9-310(a)	47
9-310(c)	57

TABLE OF STATUTES

[References are to pages.]

UNIFORM COMMERCIAL CODE (UCC)—Cont.

Sec.	Page
9-311	46; 47
9-311(a)	169
9-311(e)	169
9-312	87
9-312(b)	39
9-312(b)(3)	36; 40
9-312(c)	37
9-312(d)	37; 47
9-312(e)	35; 36
9-312(f)	39
9-312(g)	39
9-312(h)	35
9-313	37; 47; 78
9-313(a)	36; 37
9-313(c)	37; 38
9-313(d)	38; 39
9-313(e)	39
9-313(e)–(g)	47
9-313(f)	38; 39
9-313(g)	38
9-313(h)	39
9-314	47
9-314(a)	39; 40
9-314(b)	45; 46
9-315	143; 144; 145; 147
9-315(a)	142
9-315(a)(1)	29; 141
9-315(a)(2)	141; 144
9-315(b)	143
9-315(c)	144; 145
9-315(d)	144
9-315(d)(1)	145
9-315(d)(2)	144; 145
9-315(d)(3)	145
9-315(e)	145
9-316	47; 69; 107
9-316(a)	69; 70
9-316(b)	69; 70
9-316(c)	70; 71
9-316(d)	71; 72
9-316(e)	71; 72
9-316(f)	73
9-316(g)	73
9-317	130
9-317(a)	76; 77; 105
9-317(a)(1)	146; 147
9-317(a)(2)	122; 146
9-317(a)(3)	108
9-317(b)	81; 82
9-317(c)	83
9-317(d)	81; 82; 83
9-317(e)	86; 123
9-318(a)	6

UNIFORM COMMERCIAL CODE (UCC)—Cont.

Sec.	Page
9-319	6; 8
9-320	86
9-320(a)	77; 78; 79
9-320(b)	80; 81
9-320(e)	78; 81
9-321	83; 86
9-321(a)	82; 83
9-321(b)	82; 83
9-321(c)	82; 83
9-322	149
9-322(a)	75; 76; 85; 86; 87; 88
9-322(a)(1)	76; 146; 147
9-322(a)(2)	76; 146; 147
9-322(a)(3)	76; 146; 147
9-322(b)(1)	146; 147
9-322(c)(2)	148; 149
9-322(d)	149; 150
9-322(e)	149; 150
9-322(g)	75
9-323	87; 110; 88
9-323(a)	87; 88
9-323(b)	87; 88
9-323(d)	87; 88
9-323(e)	87; 88
9-323(f)	87; 88
9-323(g)	87; 88
9-324	85; 147; 148
9-324(a)	84; 85; 148
9-324(b)	84; 85; 148
9-324(d)	84; 85
9-324(g)	85; 86
9-325	142
9-326	142
9-327	89; 148
9-327–9-331	149
9-328	89; 148
9-329	89; 148
9-330	89; 148
9-330(a)	90
9-330(b)	90
9-330(d)	91
9-330(e)	90
9-330(f)	90; 91
9-332	91; 92
9-333	92; 93
9-333(a)	5
9-334	93; 94; 97
9-334(c)	93; 94
9-334(d)	94; 96; 97
9-334(e)(1)	94; 95
9-334(e)(2)	94; 97; 98
9-334(e)(3)	94; 98; 99
9-334(e)(4)	99

TS–3

UNIFORM COMMERCIAL CODE (UCC)—Cont.

Sec.	Page
9-334(f)	94; 99; 100
9-334(h)	94; 96; 97
9-335	101; 102
9-336	103; 143
9-336(a)	102
9-337	71; 72
9-338	49; 50
9-340	103; 104
9-401(a)	155; 157
9-401(b)	155; 157
9-402	151
9-403	192
9-403(b)	158
9-404(a)	158
9-405	159; 160
9-406	155; 156
9-406(a)	153; 157; 158; 159; 160
9-406(b)	158; 159
9-406(c)	159
9-406(d)	155
9-406(f)	156; 157
9-407	155
9-407(a)	155; 157
9-408	155; 156
9-408(a)	155; 157
9-408(c)	157
9-408(d)	157
9-409	155; 156
9-409(a)	155; 157
9-409(b)	157
9-501	63; 64
9-501(a)(1)(B)	95; 96
9-501(a)(2)	95
9-502	48; 53
9-502(a)	95; 96
9-502(b)	55; 95; 96
9-503	51; 52; 106
9-503(a)	50; 51; 53; 62
9-503(b)	51
9-503(c)	51; 62
9-503(d)	51
9-503(e)	51
9-504	52
9-506	52; 53; 54; 106
9-506(a)	52; 53
9-506(b)	53
9-506(c)	53
9-507	53; 54
9-507(a)	54
9-507(b)	53
9-507(c)	54
9-508	54; 55
9-509	61; 62

UNIFORM COMMERCIAL CODE (UCC)—Cont.

Sec.	Page
9-509(a)	180
9-510(a)	61
9-510(c)	59; 60
9-511	57; 58
9-512	55
9-513	56; 57; 152; 153
9-513(a)	180
9-513(b)	61
9-513(c)	180
9-514	58
9-515	56; 60; 192
9-515(a)	58; 60
9-515(b)	59; 60
9-515(c)	59; 60
9-515(d)	59; 60
9-515(e)	59; 60
9-515(f)	59; 60
9-515(g)	59; 60
9-516	62
9-516(a)	62; 63
9-516(b)	48; 49; 62; 63
9-516(b)(4)	49
9-516(b)(5)	49; 50
9-516(b)(7)	59
9-516(d)	62
9-517	62
9-518	61
9-518(c)	60
9-520(a)	48; 59
9-521(a)	50
9-521(b)	55
9-601(a)(1)	161; 162; 163
9-601(c)	162; 163
9-601(e)	162; 163
9-601(f)	162; 163
9-604	101
9-604(b)	100; 101
9-604(c)	100; 101
9-604(d)	101
9-605	180
9-607	161; 164; 178; 181
9-607(a)	158; 163
9-607(c)	164
9-608	165
9-608(a)(1)	164
9-608(a)(3)	164
9-608(a)(4)	164; 181
9-608(b)	164
9-609	161; 166
9-609(a)	165
9-609(b)(2)	165
9-609(c)	166
9-610	161; 166; 167; 168; 173; 178; 181

TABLE OF STATUTES

[References are to pages.]

UNIFORM COMMERCIAL CODE (UCC)—Cont.

Sec.	Page
9-610(a)	167
9-610(b)	167
9-610(c)	167
9-610(d)	168
9-610(e)	168
9-611	174
9-611(a)	168
9-611(b)	168; 169
9-611(c)	168; 170
9-611(c)(3)	168
9-611(d)	168; 170
9-612	169; 170
9-612(a)	169
9-612(b)	169
9-613	169; 170
9-614	169; 170; 181
9-615	170; 172; 182
9-615(a)	171
9-615(a)(1)	177; 178
9-615(c)	170
9-615(d)	171; 181
9-615(e)	171
9-615(f)	182; 183
9-616	179; 181
9-616(b)(1)	180
9-616(b)(2)	180
9-617	172; 173; 176
9-619	173
9-620	161; 176; 173; 181
9-620(a)(1)	174
9-620(a)(2)	174
9-620(b)	175
9-620(c)	174
9-620(d)	174
9-620(e)	173; 176
9-620(f)	173
9-620(g)	173; 176
9-621	174; 176
9-622	176; 177; 178
9-622(a)(1)	181
9-623	178
9-623(a)	177
9-624(a)	168; 170
9-624(b)	173
9-624(c)	177; 178
9-625	174; 178; 180; 181
9-626	181; 182; 183
9-626(a)(4)	181
9-626(a)(5)	183
9-627	167
9-627(a)	166
9-627(b)	167
9-627(c)	167

UNIFORM COMMERCIAL CODE (UCC)—Cont.

Sec.	Page
9-628	180
9-628(c)	181
9-628(d)	179
9-701	185
9-702	187
9-702(a)	185
9-702(b)	185
9-703(a)	185; 187
9-703(b)	186; 187
9-704	186
9-704(1)	187
9-704(2)	187
9-704(3)	186; 187
9-705(a)	187; 188
9-705(b)	188; 189
9-705(c)	189; 191
9-705(d)	188; 189; 191; 193
9-705(f)	193
9-706	191; 192; 193
9-706(a)	191
9-706(b)	192
9-706(c)	192
9-707	193
9-707(b)	192
9-707(e)	192
9-708	188; 189; 190; 191
9-709	188
9-709(a)	190; 191
9-709(b)	189

UNIFORM FRAUDULENT TRANSFER ACT

Sec.	Page
4	126
5	126

UNITED STATES CODE (U.S.C.)

Bankruptcy Code

Title:Sec.	Page
11:101	113
11:101(30)	137
11:101(31)	126
11:101(54)	122; 123; 124; 126
11:202	143
11:341(a)	137
11:361	119
11:362	113; 114
11:362(a)	114
11:362(b)	114
11:362(b)(3)	114
11:362(d)	117
11:362(d)(1)	118

[References are to pages.]

UNITED STATES CODE (U.S.C.)—Cont.

Bankruptcy Code—Cont.

Title:Sec.	Page
11:362(d)(2)	118
11:362(d)(3)	118
11:362(d)(4)	118
11:363	118; 120; 134
11:363(a)	119
11:363(b)(1)	118; 120
11:363(c)(1)	118; 120
11:363(c)(2)	119; 120
11:363(e)	119; 120
11:363(f)	119; 120
11:506	116
11:506(a)	114
11:506(a)(1)	114; 115; 116
11:506(a)(2)	115; 116
11:506(b)	115; 116
11:521(a)(2)(A)	137
11:521(a)(2)(B)	137
11:521(a)(6)	137
11:522	135
11:522(b)	120
11:522(f)(1)(B)	121; 122
11:522(f)(2)	122
11:522(f)(4)	122
11:524(c)	135; 136
11:524(k)	136
11:541	113
11:542	113
11:544(a)	122; 123
11:544(b)	124
11:546(b)(1)	123
11:547	126
11:547(b)	127; 128
11:547(c)	128
11:547(c)(2)	130
11:547(c)(3)	131
11:547(c)(4)	131
11:547(c)(5)	129; 132; 133
11:547(e)(2)	127; 128
11:547(e)(2)(A)	128
11:547(e)(2)(B)	128
11:547(e)(2)(C)	128
11:547(e)(3)	128; 131
11:547(f)	127
11:548	123; 124
11:552	116; 117; 144
11:552(a)	117
11:552(b)(1)	117
11:554	134; 135
11:722	134; 135
11:725	134

UNITED STATES CODE (U.S.C.)—Cont.

Bankruptcy Code—Cont.

Title:Sec.	Page
11:1122	138
11:1123	138
11:1123(b)(1)	138
11:1123(b)(5)	138
11:1124	138
11:1129	138
11:1129(a)(7)	138
11:1129(a)(8)	138
11:1129(b)	138; 139
11:1129(b)(1)	139
11:1129(b)(2)(A)	139
11:1141(a)	139
11:1322(b)	137
11:1325	137
11:1325(a)(5)	137; 138

Internal Revenue Code

Title:Sec.	Page
26:6321	105
26:6321–23	104
26:6322	104; 105
26:6323	104
26:6323(a)	105; 106; 107; 109
26:6323(b)	105
26:6323(c)	107
26:6323(c)(2)(A)	109
26:6323(c)(4)	109
26:6323(d)	110
26:6323(e)	108
26:6323(f)	106
26:6323(f)(1)(A)(ii)	106
26:6323(f)(2)	106
26:6323(f)(2)(B)	106
26:6323(h)(1)	105; 106; 109
26:6323(h)(6)	105

Food Security Act of 1985

Title:Sec.	Page
7:1631	79
7:1631(c)(1)	79; 80
7:1631(c)(2)	79
7:1631(d)	79; 80
7:1631(e)	79; 80
7:1631(e)(1)	79
7:1631(e)(2)	79
7:1631(e)(3)	79

REVENUE RULING

Rev. Rul.	Page
68-57	111

INDEX

[References are to pages.]

A

ACCESSIONS ... 101

ACCOUNTS
Collection upon default ... 163
Defenses of account debtors ... 157
Definition ... 12
Perfection ... 32
Sale of ... 5; 6; 12

ADEQUATE PROTECTION ... 119; 137

AFTER-ACQUIRED PROPERTY .. 105; 107; 128; 131

AGRICULTURAL LIENS ... 4; 63

AMENDMENT TO FINANCING STATEMENT ... 54; 192

ASSIGNMENTS
Exclusions from scope ... 14; 19
Notification of ... 153; 158
Restrictions on ... 157
Type of amendment to financing statement ... 57

ATTACHMENT
Generally ... 23
Automatic ... 27
Commingled goods ... 102
Governing law ... 65
Proceeds ... 139
Requirements ... 24
Restrictions on ... 156
Transition rules ... 185

AUTHENTICATION ... 26

AUTOMATIC PERFECTION ... 32

AUTOMATIC STAY ... 113; 117; 137

B

BANKRUPTCY
Adequate protection (See ADEQUATE PROTECTION)
Automatic stay (See AUTOMATIC STAY)
Cash collateral ... 119
Chapter 7 ... 134
Chapter 11 ... 138
Chapter 13 ... 137
Cramdown ... 138
Estate ... 113
Exemption ... 120
Fraudulent transfer ... 123

BANKRUPTCY—Cont.
Preference ... 126
Preference exceptions ... 128
Secured claim ... 114
Strong-arm clause ... 122

BREACH OF THE PEACE ... 165

BUYERS
Buyer in ordinary course of business .. 77
Buyer of consumer goods ... 80
Buyer of farm products ... 79
Buyer of goods covered by certificate of title ... 67; 71
Buyer of goods subject to unperfected security interest ... 81
Future advances ... 87; 109
Proceeds ... 147
Purchase-money security interest ... 86

C

CERTIFICATED SECURITY .. 35; 41; 67; 81

CERTIFICATE OF TITLE .. 46; 67; 69; 71; 99; 169; 174

CHATTEL PAPER
Collection upon default ... 163
Defenses of account debtors ... 158
Definition ... 13
Electronic ... 13; 39; 43; 152
Purchasers of ... 89
Sale of ... 5; 6; 13
Tangible ... 13; 43; 67; 81; 90

CLASSIFICATION OF COLLATERAL ... 11

COLLATERAL
Care of ... 151
Classification ... 11
Collateral description of ... 26
Disposition of ... 166

COMMINGLED GOODS ... 102

COMMINGLING ... 143

COMMODITY ACCOUNT ... 20; 67

COMMODITY CONTRACT ... 20; 67

CONSIGNMENT ... 6

CONSTRUCTION MORTGAGE ... 108

CONSUMER GOODS
Acceptance in satisfaction of obligation ... 173; 181

I–1

CONSUMER GOODS—Cont.
Buyer of . . . 80
Definition . . . 17
Description in consumer transaction . . . 27
Perfection of purchase-money security interest in . . . 32
Replacement of domestic appliance fixtures . . . 98
Secured party's use of . . . 152
Statutory damages . . . 179
Termination of security interest in . . . 56; 152

CONTINUATION STATEMENT . . . 58; 188; 191

CONTROL
Generally . . . 38
Deposit accounts . . . 39; 42; 88; 103; 152
Electronic chattel paper . . . 39; 43; 152
Electronic documents . . . 39; 43; 152
Investment property . . . 39; 45; 67; 88; 152
Letter-of-credit rights . . . 39; 43; 88; 152

CRAMDOWN . . . 138

D

DEBTOR
Change of . . . 28; 53
Change of name . . . 53
Definition . . . 23; 54
Errors in description . . . 52
Name . . . 50; 106
New debtor . . . 28
Original debtor . . . 28

DEPOSIT ACCOUNT
Assignment of . . . 15
Cash collateral . . . 119
Collection upon default . . . 163
Commingled proceeds in . . . 143
Control of . . . 39; 42; 88; 103; 152
Definition . . . 15
Governing law . . . 67
Priority rules . . . 88; 91; 103; 148
Termination of security interest in . . . 152

DESCRIPTION OF COLLATERAL . . . 26

DISPOSITION OF COLLATERAL . . . 166

E

ELECTRONIC CHATTEL PAPER . . . 13; 39; 43; 152

ELECTRONIC DOCUMENTS . . . 39; 43

EQUIPMENT
Definition . . . 17

EQUIPMENT—Cont.
Fixtures . . . 98
Remedies upon default . . . 165

EXCLUSIONS FROM SCOPE . . . 8

EXEMPTIONS . . . 120

F

FARM PRODUCTS . . . 4; 65; 77; 79

FEDERAL TAX LIENS . . . 104

FILING . . . 47

FINANCING STATEMENT
Contents . . . 48
Duration . . . 59
Errors . . . 49; 52
Post-filing changes . . . 53
Transition rules . . . 187
Uniform form . . . 50
When required . . . 47

FIXTURE FILING . . . 93

FIXTURES . . . 93

FOOD SECURITY ACT . . . 79

FRAUDULENT TRANSFER . . . 123

FUTURE ADVANCES . . . 86; 106; 109

G

GENERAL INTANGIBLES . . . 11; 81; 82; 155

GOODS
Accessions . . . 101
Buyer in ordinary course of business . . . 77
Commingled goods . . . 102
Consignment of . . . 6
Definition . . . 16; 22
Fixtures . . . 93
Leased (See LEASES)
Purchase-money security interests in (See PURCHASE-MONEY SECURITY INTEREST)
Retention of title as security interest . . . 2

[References are to pages.]

H

HEALTH-CARE-INSURANCE RECEIVABLES . . . 12; 155; 158

I

INSTRUMENT . . . 15; 19; 35; 67; 81; 89; 148

INVENTORY
Chattel paper as proceeds of . . . 89
Definition . . . 17
Preference exception for . . . 132
Purchase-money security interest in . . . 84; 147

INVESTMENT PROPERTY . . . 15; 20; 39; 45; 67; 81; 88; 148; 152

L

LEASES . . . 2; 3; 82; 86; 87; 155

LICENSES . . . 82

LIEN CREDITOR . . . 76; 86; 98; 122; 146

LOWEST INTERMEDIATE BALANCE RULE . . . 143

M

MANUFACTURED HOME . . . 59; 99

MORTGAGE . . . 9; 57; 59; 63; 93; 95; 96

N

NAME OF DEBTOR . . . 50; 106

NAME OF SECURED PARTY . . . 37; 51

NEGOTIABLE DOCUMENT . . 35; 37; 67; 149

NEGOTIABLE INSTRUMENT . . 19; 119; 155; 158

NEW DEBTOR . . . 28

O

OBLIGOR . . . 23; 33; 156; 164; 166; 168; 171; 173; 174; 177

P

PAYMENT INTANGIBLE
Collection upon default . . . 163; 171
Definition . . . 11

PAYMENT INTANGIBLE—Cont.
Disposition upon default . . . 181
Exclusions from scope . . . 10
Payments by account debtors . . . 158
Perfection of sale . . . 32
Restrictions on assignments of . . . 155
Sale of . . . 5; 6; 11

PERFECTION
Automatic . . . 32
Control (See CONTROL)
Defined . . . 31
Filing . . . 47
Possession/delivery . . . 36
Temporary . . . 35; 87

POSSESSION
Attachment by . . . 25
Chattel paper . . . 89
Duties of secured party in . . . 151
Governing law for possessory security interests . . . 67; 69; 70
Perfection by . . . 31; 36
Remedy for default . . . 165

POSSESSORY LIEN . . . 92

PREFERENCE . . . 126

PREFERENCE EXCEPTIONS . . . 128

PRIORITY
Accessions . . . 101
Bankruptcy . . . 122
Buyers (See BUYERS)
Commingled goods . . . 102
Control collateral . . . 88
Federal tax liens . . . 104
Fixtures . . . 93
Future advances . . . 86; 106; 109
Lessees/licensees (See LEASES; LICENSES)
Lien creditors (See LIEN CREDITOR)
Possessory liens . . . 92
Purchase-money security interests . . . 84
Purchasers of chattel paper/instruments . . 89
Right of set-off/recoupment . . . 103
Secured creditors . . . 75
Transfers of money . . . 91

PROCEEDS . . 43; 90; 107; 134; 139; 141; 164; 170; 181; 182

PROMISSORY NOTE
Collection upon default . . . 163; 171
Definition . . . 19
Disposition upon default . . . 181
Exclusions from scope . . . 10
Perfection of sale . . . 32
Restrictions on assignments of . . . 155
Sale of . . . 5; 6; 19

[References are to pages.]

PURCHASE-MONEY SECURITY INTEREST
Automatic perfection of . . . 32; 81
Avoidance of liens impairing exemptions . . 123
Definition . . . 32
Federal tax liens . . . 110
Fixtures . . . 96
Manufactured-home transaction . . . 59
Preference exception . . . 130; 137
Priority of . . . 84
Proceeds . . . 147
Redemption in bankruptcy . . . 137
Strict foreclosure . . . 173

R

REAFFIRMATION . . . 135

REDEMPTION . . . 134; 137; 177

REPOSSESSION . . . 165

S

SALE
Authorized sales . . . 141
Automatic perfection for . . . 32
Bankruptcy sales . . . 119
In scope of Article 9 . . . 1; 11; 19
Unauthorized sales . . . 141

SECONDARY OBLIGOR . . . 164; 168; 173; 174; 177; 181; 182

SECURED CLAIM . . . 114

SECURITIES ACCOUNT . . . 20; 67

SECURITY . . . 20; 23; 31; 65; 75

SECURITY AGREEMENT . . . 26

SECURITY ENTITLEMENT . . . 20; 67

SECURITY INTEREST
Assignment of . . . 57

SECURITY INTEREST—Cont.
Consignment . . . 6
Defined . . . 2
Enforceability (See ATTACHMENT)
Lease contrasted (See LEASES)
Perfection of (See PERFECTION)
Purchase-money security interest (See PURCHASE-MONEY SECURITY INTEREST)

STRICT FORECLOSURE . . . 173

STRONG-ARM CLAUSE . . . 122

SUBROGATION . . . 125

T

TANGIBLE CHATTEL PAPER . . 13; 43; 67; 81; 90

TAX LIENS . . . 104

TEMPORARY PERFECTION . . . 35; 87

TERMINATION STATEMENT . . . 55; 61; 152; 192

TRANSMITTING UTILITY . . . 59; 63

TRUSTEE IN BANKRUPTCY . . . 31; 76; 98; 113

U

UNCERTIFICATED SECURITY . . 41; 67

V

VALUE . . . 25